Talk Time

Everyday English Conversation

Student Book 3

Susan Stempleski

OXFORD

UNIVERSITY PRESS

OXFORD
UNIVERSITY PRESS

198 Madison Avenue
New York, NY 10016 USA

Great Clarendon Street, Oxford OX2 6DP UK

Oxford University Press is a department of the University of Oxford.
It furthers the University's objective of excellence in research, scholarship,
and education by publishing worldwide in

Oxford   New York

Auckland   Cape Town   Dar es Salaam   Hong Kong   Karachi
Kuala Lumpur   Madrid   Melbourne   Mexico City   Nairobi
New Delhi   Shanghai   Taipei   Toronto

With offices in

Argentina   Austria   Brazil   Chile   Czech Republic   France   Greece
Guatemala   Hungary   Italy   Japan   Poland   Portugal   Singapore
South Korea   Switzerland   Thailand   Turkey   Ukraine   Vietnam

OXFORD and OXFORD ENGLISH are registered trademarks of
Oxford University Press.

Library of Congress Cataloging-In-Publication Data

Stempleski, Susan.
  Talk time: student book / Susan Stempleski.
    p. cm.
  Contents: — [1] Book 1 — [2] Book 2 — [3] Book 3.
  ISBN-13: 978-0-19-438201-4 (Student bk. 1)
  ISBN-10: 0-19-438201-X (Student bk. 1)
  ISBN-13: 978-0-19-438208-3 (Student bk. 2)
  ISBN-10: 0-19-438208-7 (Student bk. 2)
  ISBN-13: 978-0-19-438217-5 (Student bk. 3)
  ISBN-10: 0-19-438217-6 (Student bk. 3)
  1. English language—Textbooks for foreign speakers. 2. English language—
Grammar—Problems, exercises, etc. I. Title

PE1128.S743 2006
428.2'4–dc22

                                              2006040020

No unauthorized photocopying

Market Development Director, Asia: Chris Balderston
Senior Editor: Patricia O'Neill
Editorial Assistant: Rachel Coyne
Art Director: Maj-Britt Hagsted
Senior Designer: Stacy Merlin
Art Editor: Elizabeth Blomster
Production Manager: Shanta Persaud
Production Controller: Eve Wong

ISBN: 978 0 19 438217 5 (Student Book)
ISBN: 978 0 19 439293 8 (Student Book with CD)

Printed in Hong Kong

10 9 8 7 6 5 4 3 2 1

ACKNOWLEDGMENTS

Illustrations by: Barb Bastian pp.6, 12, 30, 33, 48, 54; Kathy Baxendale pp.3,
15, 24, 36, 39, 72, 75; Janos Jatner pp.13, 21, 37, 57; Katie Mac pp.2, 11, 32,
38, 65; Marc Monés pp.16, 26, 56, 70; Pulsar Studios pp.20, 25, 34, 61; Marco
Schaaf pp. 22, 28, 67; Rob Schuster pp.9, 18, 42, 45, 60, 69, 73, 76; William
Waitzman pp.1, 31, 51, 63; Tracey Wood pp.8, 19, 49, 59.

We would like to thank the following for their permission to reproduce photographs:
Alamy: ACE STOCK, 17(cafe); Mark Baynes, 66(voting); chicagoview,
10(clouds); Chris Davies, 43(dancer); Directphoto.org, 46(Internet); f1
online, 46(airport); Paul Glendell, 66(flooded homes); Jo Hansen, 66(fire);
ImageState, 66(soccer); Dennis MacDonald, 64(flood); Vincent MacNamara,
7(lake); David Muscroft, 5(cafe); Photofusion Picture Library, 64(voting);
Profimedia.CZ.s.r.o., 55(neat); Lourens Smak, 64(art gallery); Stock
Connection, 64(handcuffs); Mark Sykes, 64(fire); Mason Trullinger, 52(tae
kwon do); Phillip Wolmuth, 66(demonstration); Corbis: Kevin Fleming,
4(potter); RainerHolz/zefa, 4(collection); Don Mason, 29(office); Simon
Marcus, 40(birthday); Patrik Giardino, 66(fashion show); Vauthey Pierre,
66(fashion show finale); Getty: Jack Hollingsworth, 50(sitting outside);
Stone, 58(go to bed late); Inmagine: Ablestock, 7(ocean), 10(snow),
52(raquetball); Asiapix, 55(mustache, bald); Bananastock, 43(surgeon),
46(meeting); Blendimages, 46(manager), 53(park); Brandxpictures, 10(rainy,
cold), 42(coins), 62(sport); Creatas,43(tennis); digitalvision, 4(team),
7(island), 43(artist, reporter, firefigher), 55(lazy, reading); 58(breakfast);
Dynamicgraphics, 4(climbing), 55(short beard); Fstop, 10(sunny); Image100,
4(camping); Imagedj, 7(hill), 10(foggy); Imagesource, 55(muscular, long
hair, shaking hands); Inspirestock, 46(meeting); 58(using alarm clock);
Medioimages,10(windy); Mikewatsonimages, 40(graduation); Mixa,
60(Japanese man); Photoalto, 58(reading newspaper); Photodisc, 7(volcano,
desert), 43(mechanic); Photos.com, 43(hairdresser), Pictureindia, 55(wavy
hair); Pixtal,7(mountain, river, stream, waterfall, forest); Purestock,
40(wedding), 62(talking on phone); Stockbyte, 60(female); Stockdisc,
52(hanging out); Thinkstock, 7(valley), 68(talking on the phone); Photoedit:
Spencer Grant, 44(shaking hands), Tom Carter, 47(bookstore); Punchstock:
digitalvision, 43(cashier); Superstock: age footstock, 43(photographer),
52,(concert), 58(bike riding); BananaStock, 40(dinner party); Blend
Images, 58(wake up early); Digital Vision Ltd., 43(police officer); Greg
Martin, 64(demonstration); Image Source, 46(writing report), 71(chatting);
Kwame Zikomo, 40(New Years); Pixtal, 35(chatting), 68(talking on the
phone); Purestock, 23(cafeteria); Stock Image, 14(chatting); Stockdisc,
10(hot), 62(talking on the phone), The Copyright Group, 40(Anniversary),
ThinkStock, 43(manager), 52(horseback riding).

*We would like to thank the following for their permission to reproduce photographs on
the cover:* Corbis (clock); Inmagine (couple); Getty (background).

The publishers would like to thank the following for their help in developing this series:
Mei-ho Chiu, Taiwan; Kirsten Duckett, Seoul, South Korea; Laura MacGregor,
Tokyo, Japan; Andrew Zitzmann, Osaka, Japan.

*The publishers would also like to thank the following OUP staff for their support and
assistance:* Ted Yoshioka.

Contents

Scope and sequence

Unit	Theme	Grammar	Vocabulary
1 page 1	Talking about yourself and others: Describing character Free-time activities	The simple present vs. the present continuous; the simple past vs. the present perfect	Adjectives for personality and character; hobbies and sports
2 page 7	Comparing places: Geography Weather	Comparative forms of adjectives; superlative forms of adjectives	Adjectives for describing places; weather words
3 page 13	Everyday activities Life experiences	The past continuous; the simple past vs. the past continuous	Everyday activities; important life events
4 page 19	School subjects At school	Adjectives ending in -*ing* and -*ed*; the present perfect with *already*, *never*, *still*, and *yet*	School subjects; adjectives for describing feelings
5 page 25	Phone messages Favors and requests	Requests with *can*, *will*, *could*, and *would*; *Would you mind...?*	Types of phone messages, requests, and offers; favors and requests
6 page 31	Wishes Opinions	Verb forms after *wish*; *too* and *enough*	Wishes for life changes; topics to express opinions about
7 page 37	Customs Events and celebrations	*It* + infinitive; gerunds as subjects; time clauses with *before*, *when*, and *after*	Cultural customs; special occasions
8 page 43	Jobs At work	The present perfect with *how long*; *since* and *for*; verb + infinitive, verb + gerund, and phrase + gerund	Jobs and occupations; different tasks and work activities
9 page 49	Recent activities Leisure activities	The present perfect continuous; the present perfect continuous vs. the present perfect	Daily activities and routines; leisure activities
10 page 55	Describing people Everyday habits	*Used to*; the simple past with *how long*	Describing appearance and character; habits
11 page 61	Stories In the news	Reported speech; *while* and *then* in clauses	Different types of stories; news events
12 page 67	Before you travel Travel experiences	*Have to*, *have got to*, and *must*; the present perfect for time continuing up to the present	Preparing to travel; travel experiences

To the student

Welcome to *Talk Time*. Let's take a look at a unit.

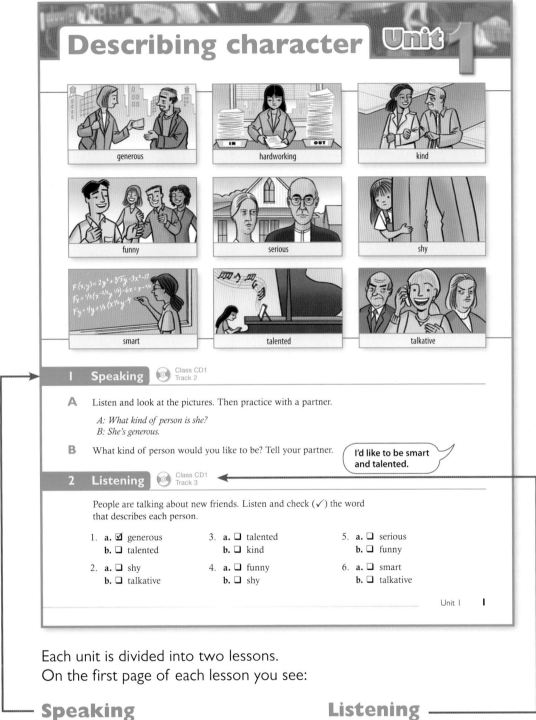

Each unit is divided into two lessons.
On the first page of each lesson you see:

Speaking

First you practice the new vocabulary for this lesson. You will listen to the CD and look at the pictures. Then you practice using the new words with a classmate.

Listening

In this section, you listen to the vocabulary in short conversations and answer some questions.

On the second page of each lesson you see:

Grammar

In this section, you see the grammar focus for this lesson. You listen to the CD and then practice the grammar.

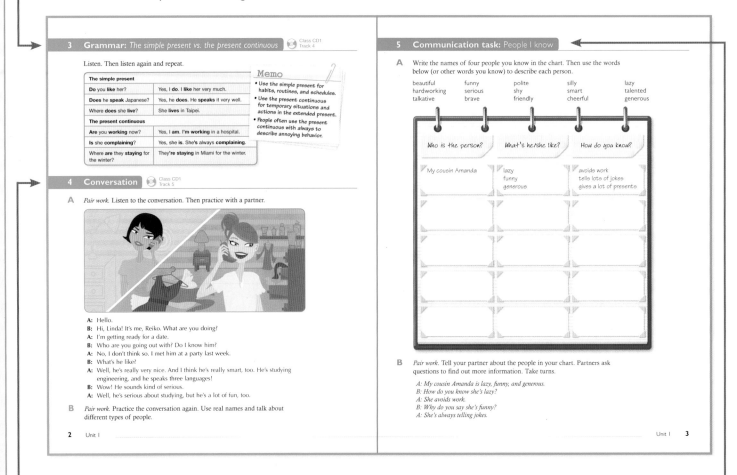

3 Grammar: *The simple present vs. the present continuous* Class CD1 Track 4

Listen. Then listen again and repeat.

The simple present	
Do you **like** her?	Yes, I **do**. I **like** her very much.
Does he **speak** Japanese?	Yes, he **does**. He **speaks** it very well.
Where **does** she **live**?	She **lives** in Taipei.
The present continuous	
Are you **working** now?	Yes, I **am**. I**'m working** in a hospital.
Is she **complaining**?	Yes, she is. She**'s** always **complaining**.
Where **are** they **staying** for the winter?	They**'re staying** in Miami for the winter.

Memo
• Use the simple present for habits, routines, and schedules.
• Use the present continuous for temporary situations and actions in the extended present.
• People often use the present continuous with *always* to describe annoying behavior.

4 Conversation Class CD1 Track 5

A *Pair work.* Listen to the conversation. Then practice with a partner.

A: Hello.
B: Hi, Linda! It's me, Reiko. What are you doing?
A: I'm getting ready for a date.
B: Who are you going out with? Do I know him?
A: No, I don't think so. I met him at a party last week.
B: What's he like?
A: Well, he's really very nice. And I think he's really smart, too. He's studying engineering, and he speaks three languages!
B: Wow! He sounds kind of serious.
A: Well, he's serious about studying, but he's a lot of fun, too.

B *Pair work.* Practice the conversation again. Use real names and talk about different types of people.

2   Unit 1

5 Communication task: People I know

A Write the names of four people you know in the chart. Then use the words below (or other words you know) to describe each person.

beautiful   funny   polite   silly   lazy
hardworking   serious   shy   smart   talented
talkative   brave   friendly   cheerful   generous

Who is the person?	What's he/she like?	How do you know?
My cousin Amanda	lazy / funny / generous	avoids work / tells lots of jokes / gives a lot of presents

B *Pair work.* Tell your partner about the people in your chart. Partners ask questions to find out more information. Take turns.

A: My cousin Amanda is lazy, funny, and generous.
B: How do you know she's lazy?
A: She avoids work.
B: Why do you say she's funny?
A: She's always telling jokes.

Unit 1   **3**

Conversation

In this section, you listen to a conversation and then practice with a partner. This lets you practice the vocabulary and grammar of the lesson in a larger context. It also lets you use your own information.

On the third page of each lesson you see:

Communication task

In this section, you practice the language of the lesson with a partner or a small group. This section lets you use your own information to speak more freely about the topic. Sometimes you and your partner will look at the same page, and sometimes you will look at different pages.

Other things you see in the unit:

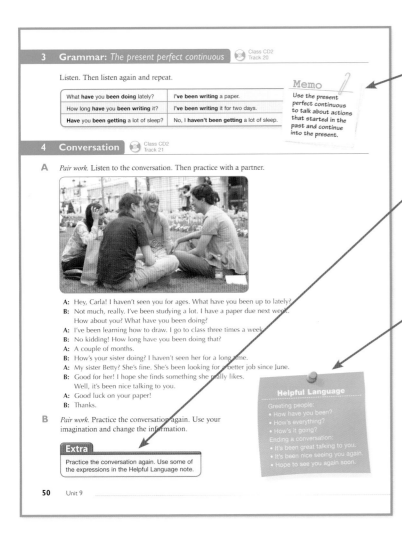

3 Grammar: *The present perfect continuous* Class CD2 Track 20

Listen. Then listen again and repeat.

What **have** you **been doing** lately?	I**'ve been writing** a paper.
How long **have** you **been writing** it?	I**'ve been writing** it for two days.
Have you **been getting** a lot of sleep?	No, I **haven't been getting** a lot of sleep.

Memo
Use the present perfect continuous to talk about actions that started in the past and continue into the present.

4 Conversation Class CD2 Track 21

A *Pair work.* Listen to the conversation. Then practice with a partner.

A: Hey, Carla! I haven't seen you for ages. What have you been up to lately?
B: Not much, really. I've been studying a lot. I have a paper due next week. How about you? What have you been doing?
A: I've been learning how to draw. I go to class three times a week.
B: No kidding! How long have you been doing that?
A: A couple of months.
B: How's your sister doing? I haven't seen her for a long time.
A: My sister Betty? She's fine. She's been looking for a better job since June.
B: Good for her! I hope she finds something she really likes. Well, it's been nice talking to you.
A: Good luck on your paper!
B: Thanks.

B *Pair work.* Practice the conversation again. Use your imagination and change the information.

Extra
Practice the conversation again. Use some of the expressions in the Helpful Language note.

Helpful Language
Greeting people:
• How have you been?
• How's everything?
• How's it going?
Ending a conversation:
• It's been great talking to you.
• It's been nice seeing you again.
• Hope to see you again soon.

50   Unit 9

Memo

The *Memo* reminds you about rules of English that are different from your language, for example, contractions. The language in the Memo will help you complete the activities.

Extra

Sometimes you will see an *Extra* activity. This lets you practice more with the same language from the activity.

Helpful Language

The *Helpful Language* note gives you questions or phrases that will help you complete the activities. They provide cues you can use to keep talking longer with your partner.

CD Icon

The CD icon tells you that this activity is recorded on the audio CD, and your teacher may play it in class in order for you to do the activity.

Check your English

Check your English

Unit 1

A Vocabulary

Complete the sentences. Use the words below.

| band | camping | generous | serious |
| shy | talented | talkative | team |

1. We went ____camping____ in the mountains on our last vacation.

2. He never smiles or tells a joke. He's a very _____ person.

3. She's a very _____ musician. Sh...

At the back of the book, there is a review page called *Check your English*. This page gives you a chance to review the language from the Unit.

Every lesson gives you time to listen to English, and time to talk with your classmates. *Talk Time* will help you increase your vocabulary and improve grammatical accuracy. I hope you enjoy studying with *Talk Time*. Good luck!

Describing character

generous

hardworking

kind

funny

serious

shy

smart

talented

talkative

1 Speaking
 Class CD1 Track 2

A Listen and look at the pictures. Then practice with a partner.

A: What kind of person is she?
B: She's generous.

B What kind of person would you like to be? Tell your partner.

> I'd like to be smart and talented.

2 Listening
 Class CD1 Track 3

People are talking about new friends. Listen and check (✓) the word that describes each person.

1. **a.** ☑ generous
    b. ❑ talented

2. **a.** ❑ shy
    b. ❑ talkative

3. **a.** ❑ talented
    b. ❑ kind

4. **a.** ❑ funny
    b. ❑ shy

5. **a.** ❑ serious
    b. ❑ funny

6. **a.** ❑ smart
    b. ❑ talkative

Listen. Then listen again and repeat.

The simple present	
Do you **like** her?	Yes, I **do**. I **like** her very much.
Does he **speak** Japanese?	Yes, he **does**. He **speaks** it very well.
Where **does** she **live**?	She **lives** in Taipei.
The present continuous	
Are you **working** now?	Yes, I **am**. I'**m working** in a hospital.
Is she **complaining**?	Yes, she **is**. She'**s** always **complaining**.
Where **are** they **staying** for the winter?	They'**re staying** in Miami for the winter.

> **Memo**
> • Use the simple present for habits, routines, and schedules.
> • Use the present continuous for temporary situations and actions in the extended present.
> • People often use the present continuous with *always* to describe annoying behavior.

4 Conversation Class CD1 Track 5

A *Pair work.* Listen to the conversation. Then practice with a partner.

A: Hello.

B: Hi, Linda! It's me, Reiko. What are you doing?

A: I'm getting ready for a date.

B: Who are you going out with? Do I know him?

A: No, I don't think so. I met him at a party last week.

B: What's he like?

A: Well, he's really very nice. And I think he's really smart, too. He's studying engineering, and he speaks three languages!

B: Wow! He sounds kind of serious.

A: Well, he's serious about studying, but he's a lot of fun, too.

B *Pair work.* Practice the conversation again. Use real names and talk about different types of people.

A   Write the names of four people you know in the chart. Then use the words below (or other words you know) to describe each person.

beautiful   funny   polite   silly   lazy
hardworking   serious   shy   smart   talented
talkative   brave   friendly   cheerful   generous

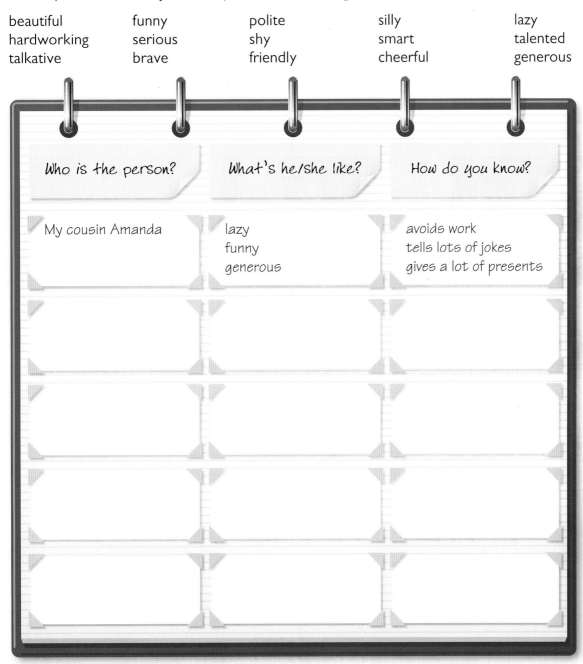

Who is the person?	What's he/she like?	How do you know?
My cousin Amanda	lazy funny generous	avoids work tells lots of jokes gives a lot of presents

B   *Pair work.* Tell your partner about the people in your chart. Partners ask questions to find out more information. Take turns.

A: *My cousin Amanda is lazy, funny, and generous.*
B: *How do you know she's lazy?*
A: *She avoids work.*
B: *Why do you say she's funny?*
A: *She's always telling jokes.*

Free-time activities

play in a band

play on a team

do arts and crafts

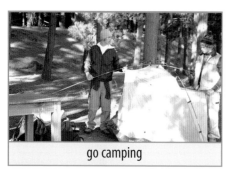
go camping

collect things

go rock climbing

6 Speaking
Class CD1 Track 6

A Listen and look at the pictures. Then practice with a partner.

A: What do they do in their free time?
B: They play in a band.

B Which of these activities do you do? Which ones don't you do? Tell your partner.

> I play in a band. I don't…

7 Listening
Class CD1 Track 7

A People are talking about free-time activities. Which activities are they talking about? Listen and number the activities from 1 to 6.

__1__ going rock climbing   ____ playing on a team   ____ doing arts and crafts
____ going camping   ____ collecting comic books   ____ playing in a band

B Listen again. Are the people talking about things they do *now* or things they did *in the past*? Check (✓) the correct answer.

1. **a.** ❑ now
   b. ❑ in the past

2. **a.** ❑ now
   b. ❑ in the past

3. **a.** ❑ now
   b. ❑ in the past

4. **a.** ❑ now
   b. ❑ in the past

5. **a.** ❑ now
   b. ❑ in the past

6. **a.** ❑ now
   b. ❑ in the past

8 Grammar: *The simple past vs. the present perfect*

A Listen. Then listen again and repeat.

The simple past	
When **did** you **graduate** from high school?	I **graduated** last year.
What **did** you **do** last weekend?	I **went** to the movies.
When **did** you last **visit** a museum?	I **visited** a museum last month.
The present perfect	
Have you ever **played** tennis?	Yes, I **have**. I**'ve played** many times.
Have you ever **had** a pet?	No, I **haven't**. I**'ve** never **had** one.
How often **have** you **eaten** sushi?	I**'ve eaten** it once.

Memo
• Use the simple past for a specific event in the past.
• Use the present perfect for an indefinite time in the past.

B *Pair work.* Ask your partner questions about his or her past experiences. Ask follow-up questions to find out more information.

Have you ever had a pet?   Yes, I have.   What kind of pet did you have?

9 Conversation

A *Pair work.* Listen to the conversation. Then practice with a partner.

A: Have you ever eaten Thai food?
B: No, I haven't tried it. Have you?
A: Yes, I have.
B: Where did you have it?
A: I had it when I was in Thailand.
B: When did you go to Thailand?
A: Two years ago. I went there with my parents.
B: Did you have a good time?
A: Yes, I did. It's a very interesting country.
B: And what about Thai food? Did you like it?
A: Oh, yeah. It was a little spicy, but I loved it.

B *Pair work.* Practice the conversation again. Talk about different kinds of food and places

Extra

Complete these questions in your own words. Then ask your partner the questions. Ask follow-up questions with *where*, *what*, and *who* to find out more information.

Have you ever...?   How often have you...?   When did you last...?

A *Class activity.* Ask questions with *Have you ever...?* Find one classmate for each activity. Write your classmates' names and any extra information.

> A: *Have you ever done arts and crafts?*
> B: *Yes, I have.*
> A: *What kind of arts and crafts did you do?*
> B: *I made jewelry.*
> A: *When...?*

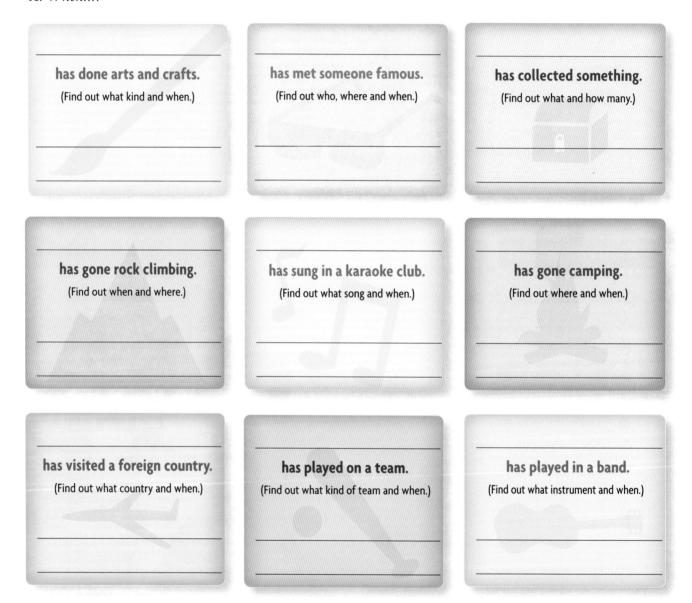

_____ has done arts and crafts.
(Find out what kind and when.)
_____

_____ has met someone famous.
(Find out who, where and when.)
_____

_____ has collected something.
(Find out what and how many.)
_____

_____ has gone rock climbing.
(Find out when and where.)
_____

_____ has sung in a karaoke club.
(Find out what song and when.)
_____

_____ has gone camping.
(Find out where and when.)
_____

_____ has visited a foreign country.
(Find out what country and when.)
_____

_____ has played on a team.
(Find out what kind of team and when.)
_____

_____ has played in a band.
(Find out what instrument and when.)
_____

B *Group work.* Tell your partners about your classmates' hobbies. Tell as many details as you can.

Marta has done arts and crafts. She made jewelry when she was in high school.

Geography

mountain

volcano

river

island

lake

valley

stream

waterfall

desert

hill

forest

ocean

---

1 Speaking Class CD1
Track 10

A Listen and look at the pictures. Then practice with a partner.

> A: *What's this?*
> B: *It's a mountain.*

B Have you seen any of these things?
Which ones? Tell your partner.

> I've seen many mountains.
> For example, Mount…

2 Listening Class CD1
Track 11

People are talking about things they saw on their vacations. What did they see?
Listen and check (✓) the correct answer.

1. **a.** ❑ a mountain
   b. ❑ a stream

2. **a.** ❑ a valley
   b. ❑ a river

3. **a.** ❑ a forest
   b. ❑ a volcano

4. **a.** ❑ an island
   b. ❑ a waterfall

5. **a.** ❑ a desert
   b. ❑ a lake

6. **a.** ❑ an ocean
   b. ❑ a hill

Listen. Then listen again and repeat.

Which desert is **larger**, the Sahara or the Gobi?
The Sahara is **larger than** the Gobi.
Which river is **longer**, the Amazon or the Nile?
The Nile is **longer than** the Amazon.
Which mountain is **more famous**, Everest or K2?
I think Everest is **more famous**.

Memo

many → more
far → farther
hot → hotter
dry → drier
crowded → more crowded
beautiful → more beautiful

4 **Conversation**   Class CD1
Track 13

A *Pair work.* Listen to the conversation. Then practice with a partner.

A: What are you doing, Koichi?

B: I'm trying to finish this geography quiz, but I'm not sure about all the answers.

A: Well, maybe I can help. I'm pretty good at geography. Go ahead. Ask me a question.

B: OK. Here's one. Which ocean is larger, the Indian or the Arctic?

A: That's easy. The Indian Ocean is a lot bigger than the Arctic Ocean.

B: Thanks! Now, how about this question? Which country is more mountainous, Spain or Switzerland?

A: I know the answer to that one, too. It's Switzerland!

B: Gee, you really *are* good at geography.

A: Thanks! But, you know, my sister is even better!

B *Pair work.* Practice the conversation again. Use real names and ask and answer questions about different places.

Extra

Take turns comparing places and things in your country or city.
Seoul is larger than Pusan.
Mount Fuji is higher than Mount Hodaka.

Student A looks at this page. Student B looks at page 73.

A *Pair work.* Look at the web page below. Your partner will ask you questions about items on the web page. Use the information to answer your partner's questions.

> *B: Which continent is bigger, Africa or Asia?*
> *A: Asia is bigger than Africa.*

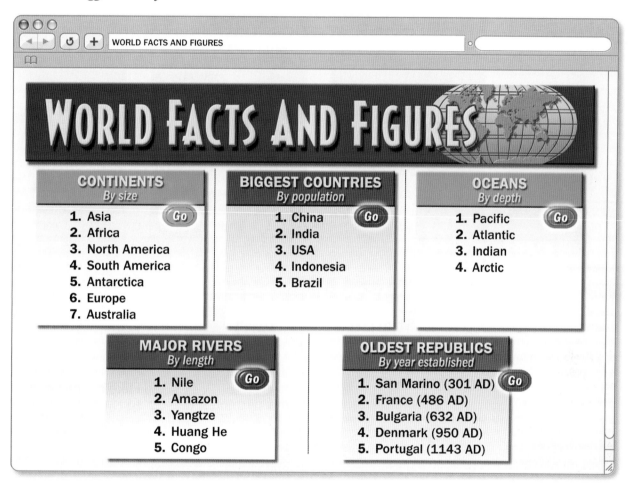

B *Pair work.* Ask your partner the questions in the list below. Use the comparative form of the adjectives in parentheses.

> *A: Which ocean is ___bigger___, the Pacific or the Atlantic? (big)*
> *B: The Pacific is bigger than the Atlantic.*

1. Which continent's population is _____, Asia's or Africa's? (large)

2. Which mountain is _____, Makalu or Annapurna? (high)

3. Which ocean is _____, the Indian or the Arctic? (small)

4. Which country is _____, Slovakia or Palau? (young)

5. Which country is _____, the Czech Republic or East Timor? (old)

6. Which city is _____, Kano or Tangail? (crowded)

Weather

sunny

cloudy

rainy

cold

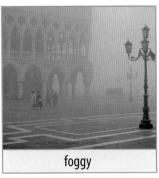
foggy

snowy

windy

hot

6 Speaking
Class CD1
Track 14

A Listen and look at the pictures. Then practice with a partner.

A: How's the weather today?
B: It's sunny.

B What's your favorite kind of weather? Why? Tell your partner.

> I like sunny weather because I can go to the beach.

7 Listening
Class CD1
Track 15

A Listen to the weather reports. Check (✓) the answer that does *not* describe the weather today.

1. **a.** ❑ It's snowing.
   b. ❑ It's cold.
   c. ❑ It's windy.

2. **a.** ❑ It's raining.
   b. ❑ It's cloudy.
   c. ❑ It's windy.

3. **a.** ❑ It's cold.
   b. ❑ It's snowing.
   c. ❑ It's hot.

B Listen again. Is tomorrow's weather going to be better or worse? Check (✓) the correct answer.

1. ❑ better
   ❑ worse

2. ❑ better
   ❑ worse

3. ❑ better
   ❑ worse

A Listen. Then listen again and repeat.

> Which is **the coldest** continent in the world?
>
> Antarctica is **the coldest**.
>
> Which planet is **the hottest**: Mars, Saturn, or Venus?
>
> Venus is **the hottest**.
>
> Which city has **the driest** climate: London, Cairo, or New York?
>
> Cairo has **the driest** climate.

Memo

nice → the nicest
sunny → the sunniest
rainy → the rainiest
famous → the most famous
beautiful → the most beautiful
good → the best
bad → the worst

B *Pair work.* Take turns making sentences about things and places in your country. Use superlative forms of adjectives.

> I think Haeundae is the most beautiful beach in Korea.

9 **Conversation** Class CD1
Track 17

A *Pair work.* Listen to the conversation. Then practice with a partner.

A: Hello?

B: Hi, Lea. It's Sarah.

A: Sarah! Where are you? I thought you were on vacation.

B: I am. I'm calling you from Mexico.

A: Is everything OK?

B: Everything's fine. Mexico is the friendliest and most beautiful country I've ever visited.

A: How's the weather?

B: Excellent. This is the best season to visit. The most beautiful weather is right now, in winter.

A: It's not cold?

B: Not at all. It's been sunny and warm every day, and it looks like today is going to be the warmest day yet.

A: Well, I'm really glad you're having a good time.

B *Pair work.* Practice the conversation again. Use real names and talk about different places.

A Look at the chart. Use the words in parentheses to make questions about a city. Use superlative forms of adjectives.

	YOUR ANSWERS	YOUR PARTNER'S ANSWERS
(What / name / city) What's the name of the city?		
(What / hot / month) What's the hottest month?		
(What / cold / month)		
(What / rainy / month)		
(What / interesting / place)		
(What / beautiful / place)		
(What / good / university)		
(What / expensive / restaurant)		
(What / crowded / section)		
(What / quiet / place)		

B Think about a city you know well. Answer each question, making short notes in the chart.

C *Pair work.* Ask your partner the questions. Write the answers in the chart. Ask other questions to get more information. Take turns.

D *Class activity.* Take turns. Tell the class what city your partner talked about and what you learned from your partner about that city.

Everyday activities

get on the subway

get off a bus

withdraw money

feed a pet

practice the violin

visit a friend

clean one's room

take a walk

play basketball

wait for a bus

do homework

get dressed

1 Speaking
Class CD1
Track 18

A Listen and look at the pictures. Then practice with a partner.

> A: *What was she doing at this time yesterday?*
> B: *She was getting on the subway.*

B What were you doing at this time yesterday? Tell your partner. (**At this time yesterday, I was...**)

2 Listening
Class CD1
Track 19

People are talking about past activities. What activities are they talking about? Listen and number the activities from 1 to 6.

_____ getting on a bus   _____ waiting for a bus   _____ withdrawing money
_____ feeding a pet   _____ getting on the subway   _____ visiting a friend

3 Grammar: *The past continuous*

Class CD1
Track 20

Listen. Then listen again and repeat.

Sam and I **were playing** basketball at ten o'clock last night.
I **was doing** homework at this time yesterday.
They **were living** in Canada in 2005.
He **was studying** in New Zealand last year.

Memo

Use the past continuous for something that was happening at a particular time in the past. These verbs are not usually used in continuous tenses: *have, know, like, love, need, seem, want.*

4 Conversation

Class CD1
Track 21

A   *Pair work.* Listen to the conversation. Then practice with a partner.

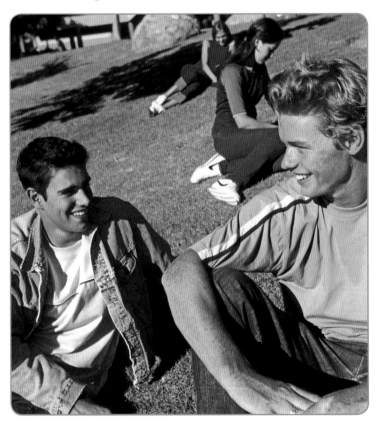

A: Hey, Toby. I called you last night, but you didn't answer your phone.

B: That's funny. I was home all evening. What time did you call?

A: Around eight o'clock.

B: Oh, yeah. I was taking a walk. Why did you call?

B: Randy and I were playing volleyball, and we wanted to know if you could join us.

A: Did you leave a message?

B: I tried to, but your voice mail wasn't working.

A: Really? I hope it's working now.

B   *Pair work.* Practice the conversation again. Use real names. Change the time of the phone call and the reason for not answering.

Extra

Take turns using the following verbs in the past continuous to make sentences about what you were doing or not doing at different times yesterday.

play	watch	practice	visit
fix	wait	get	go

I was waiting for the bus at seven o'clock yesterday morning.

A Use the time expressions below to write six statements about yourself,
some true and some false. Use the past continuous.

I was doing homework at nine o'clock last night.

I was living in Hong Kong in 2004.

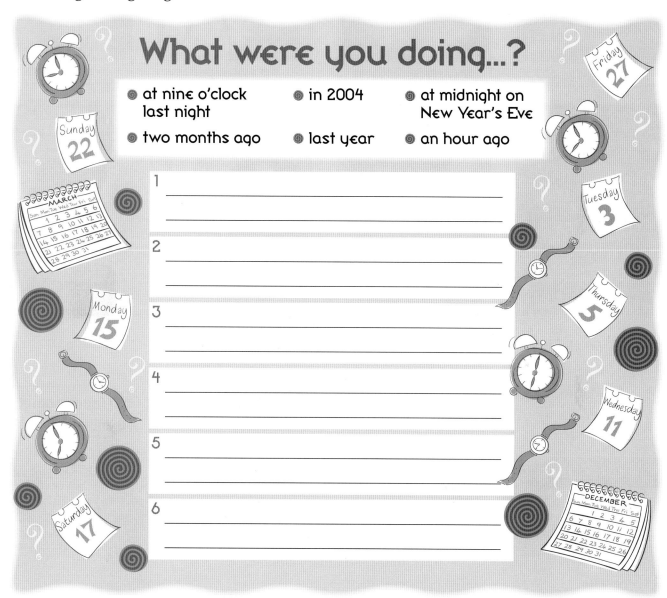

What were you doing...?

- at nine o'clock last night
- in 2004
- at midnight on New Year's Eve
- two months ago
- last year
- an hour ago

1 _____

2 _____

3 _____

4 _____

5 _____

6 _____

B *Pair work.* Take turns reading the sentences you wrote. Partners ask questions
to find out if each other's sentences are true or false.

A: What were you doing at nine o'clock last night?
B: I was studying.
A: Where were you studying?
B: I was studying at the library.
A: I don't believe you. The library closes at eight o'clock.
B: That's right. I wasn't studying. I was watching TV at home.

Life experiences

find something valuable

do something dangerous

visit a special place

meet someone famous

win a prize

get engaged

get married

have an accident

6 Speaking
Class CD1 Track 22

A Listen and look at the pictures. Then practice with a partner.

A: What did he do?
B: He found something valuable.

B Which of these things have happened to you? When? Tell your partner.

> I found something valuable last year.

7 Listening
Class CD1 Track 23

A People are talking about what happened to them. Listen and write the correct letter.

1. She ___	**a.** found something valuable.
2. He ___	**b.** met someone famous.
3. She ___	**c.** did something dangerous.
4. He ___	**d.** had an accident.

B Listen again. Are these sentences true or false? Check (✓) the correct answer.

	True	False
1. She was living in Chicago when it happened.	❑	❑
2. He was visiting California when it happened.	❑	❑
3. She was listening to her MP3 player when it happened.	❑	❑
4. He was watching a movie when it happened.	❑	❑

A Listen. Then listen again and repeat.

I **was working** in a bank when I **met** him.
She **was living** in Seoul when she **won** a prize in a contest.
He **had** an accident while he **was driving** to work.
It **started** to rain while they **were waiting** for the bus.

Memo

Use the simple past for completed actions.

Use the past continuous for actions in progress in the past.

B *Pair work.* Ask and answer questions beginning with the phrases below.

Where were you living when...?
What were you doing when...?
How did you feel when...?

Where were you living when you started school?

I was living in Seoul.

A *Pair work.* Listen to the conversation. Then practice with a partner.

A: So tell me, Jenny. How did you meet your husband? Did you meet him in Japan?

B: Oh, no. I was living in Vancouver when I met Alex.

A: Vancouver? When did you live in Vancouver?

B: I lived there for two years, from 2000 to 2002.

A: That's interesting. Well, go on. Tell me more.

B: One day, I was carrying some heavy boxes into my apartment. Alex was sitting on the front steps of the building, and he offered to help me.

A: Did you like him right away?

B: Oh, yes. I liked him a lot. He seemed really nice.

B *Pair work.* Practice the conversation again. Use real names and talk about how you met important people in your life: your husband, wife, boyfriend, girlfriend, or best friend.

A Think of a true story about yourself. Use one of the ideas in the list below, or an idea of your own. Use the chart to make notes about what happened.

Story ideas: A time you...
- won a prize
- helped someone
- found something valuable
- did something dangerous
- met someone famous

- tried something new
- visited a special place
- had an accident
- lost something
- fell in love

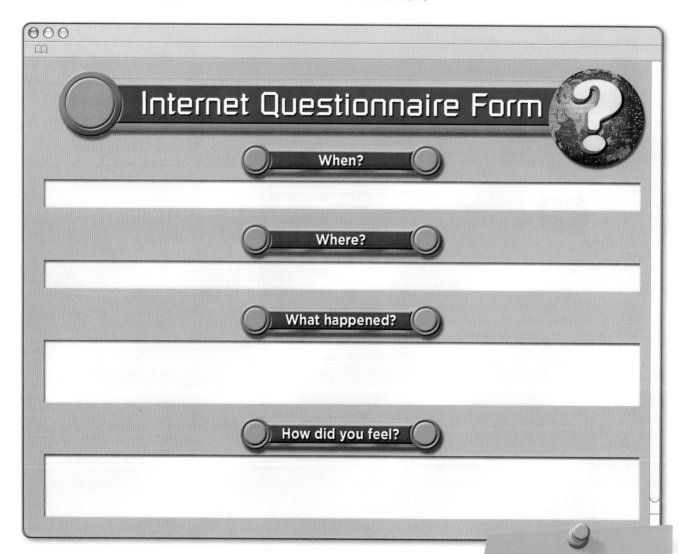

Internet Questionnaire Form

When?

Where?

What happened?

How did you feel?

B *Group work.* Use your notes to tell your story to the group. Use the simple past and the past continuous to describe what happened. Take turns. Group members express interest and ask questions to find out more information.

When I was visiting Hawaii, I did something dangerous. I...

Helpful Language

Expressing interest:
- And?
- Really?
- And then?

School subjects

biology

computer science

music

art

chemistry

history

math

languages

---

1   Speaking
Class CD1
Track 26

A   Listen and look at the pictures. Then practice with a partner.

> A: *What are they studying?*
> B: *They're studying biology.*

B   What are your favorite subjects? Tell your partner.

My favorite subjects are...

---

2   Listening
Class CD1
Track 27

People are talking about subjects they are studying. Listen and write
the correct letter.

1. She ____
2. He ____
3. She ____
4. He ____
5. She ____

a. is studying two languages.
b. says the history class is boring.
c. thinks biology is interesting.
d. thinks the music teacher is amazing.
e. isn't studying any languages this semester.

Listen. Then listen again and repeat.

Adjectives ending in -ing

History is **interesting**.

That book was **boring**.

This problem is **confusing**.

Adjectives ending in –ing describe things or people that cause a feeling.

Adjectives ending in -ed

I'm **interested** in history.

I was **bored** by that book.

I'm **confused** by this problem.

Memo
Adjectives ending in –ed usually describe how a person feels.

4 **Conversation** Class CD1 Track 29

A   *Pair work.* Listen to the conversation. Then practice with a partner.

A: Is that your art history book? It looks interesting.

B: It *is*. I'm interested in modern art. I love this class.

A: How's the teacher?

A: He's amazing. His name's Mr. Pang. He's an exciting teacher. The class is never boring.

A: I'm interested in art. Maybe I should take that course. To tell you the truth, I was bored in the art class I took last semester.

B: Well, try this class. I'm sure you won't be disappointed.

B   *Pair work.* Practice the conversation again. Use different school subjects.

Extra

Choose adjectives from the list below to complete the following sentences. Then use the sentences to interview your partner. Ask questions with *who, where, what, when, why,* and *how.*

amazing – amazed   disappointing – disappointed
exciting – excited   shocking – shocked
surprising – surprised

Talk about a/an _____ experience.

Tell me about a time you were _____.

A   Look at the pictures. How would you describe each picture? Use the *–ing* and *–ed* forms of the verbs below.

| amaze | annoy | confuse | excite | shock |
| amuse | bore | disappoint | interest | surprise |

The man is confused. The directions are confusing.

B   *Pair work.* Point to a picture and make a sentence using the *–ing* or *–ed* form of one of the verbs in the list above. Partners ask a follow-up question to continue the conversation. Take turns.

> *A: The man is confused.*
> *B: Why is he confused?*
> *A: The directions are confusing.*

At school

miss a class

study for a test

take a test

ask questions

take notes

fail a test

6 Speaking
Class CD1
Track 30

A Listen and look at the pictures. Then practice with a partner.

A: What did he do yesterday?
B: He missed a class.

B What are some things you've done at school this week? Tell your partner.

> I haven't missed a class, and I've...

7 Listening
Class CD1
Track 31

A People are talking about their classes. Which question are they answering?
Listen and number the questions from 1 to 6.

_____ Do you ask questions in class?
_____ Do you take notes in class?
_____ Do you take a lot of tests?

_____ Have you started studying for the test yet?
_____ Have you ever failed a test?
_____ How often do you miss a class?

B Listen again. Check (✓) the best response.

1. **a.** ❑ OK. See you later.
   b. ❑ I don't either.

2. **a.** ❑ I'm glad you like them.
   b. ❑ Why don't you like them?

3. **a.** ❑ I agree.
   b. ❑ Me, too.

4. **a.** ❑ That's too bad.
   b. ❑ Me, neither.

5. **a.** ❑ I think so, too.
   b. ❑ So do I.

6. **a.** ❑ I agree.
   b. ❑ That's too bad.

A Listen. Then listen again and repeat.

The present perfect
I've **already taken** an English test.
She **has never attended** class.
He **still hasn't started** studying for the test.
Have you **done** your homework **yet**?

Memo

- Use *already* to say you've completed something.
- Use *never* for things that did not happen at any time in the past.
- Use *still* and *yet* in negative sentences to say something hasn't happened, but may happen in the future.
- Use *yet* for questions about things that happened at any time up to the present.

B *Pair work.* Take turns making sentences about your experiences in English class. Say what you and your classmates have and haven't done. Use *already, still, never,* or *yet.*

> I've never fallen asleep in class.

> We haven't taken a test yet.

A *Pair work.* Listen to the conversation. Then practice with a partner.

A: The semester started only two weeks ago, and I've already taken three tests. I've never studied so much.

B: Really? I haven't had any tests yet. But you and I both have one on Friday—a math test.

A: Yeah, I know. And I think it's going to be difficult. Do you want to get together to study for it?

B: Sure. When do you want to meet?

A: How about tomorrow? I can't do it today. I'm writing an essay for my English class, and I haven't finished it yet.

B: OK, let's get together tomorrow.

B *Pair work.* Practice the conversation again. Change the subjects and other information.

A Look at the questions below. Which five would you like to talk about? Check (✓) the boxes.

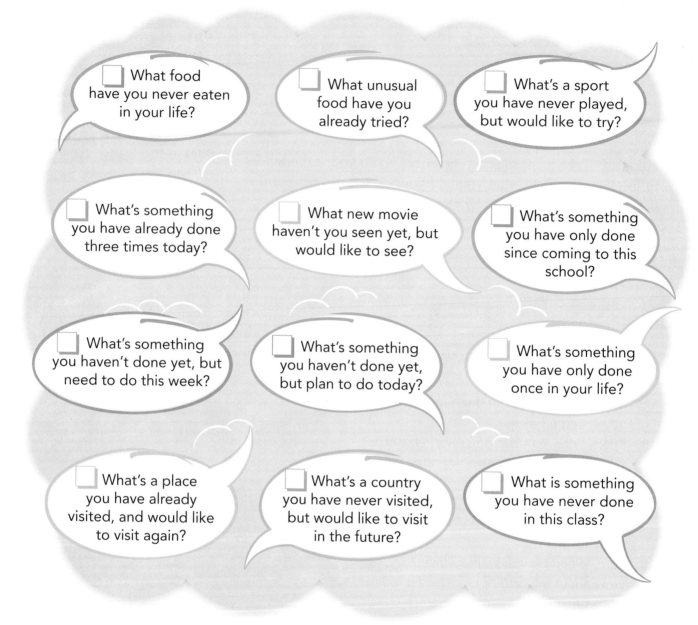

What food have you never eaten in your life?

What unusual food have you already tried?

What's a sport you have never played, but would like to try?

What's something you have already done three times today?

What new movie haven't you seen yet, but would like to see?

What's something you have only done since coming to this school?

What's something you haven't done yet, but need to do this week?

What's something you haven't done yet, but plan to do today?

What's something you have only done once in your life?

What's a place you have already visited, and would like to visit again?

What's a country you have never visited, but would like to visit in the future?

What is something you have never done in this class?

B *Pair work.* Look at your partner's book. Take turns asking each other the questions you have checked. Listen to your partner's answers. Ask follow-up questions to find out more information.

A: *What food have you never eaten in your life?*
B: *I've never eaten meat.*
A: *Why not?*
B: *My family is vegetarian.*

Helpful Language

• Why not?
• Why haven't you…?
• When did you…?
• Why would you like to…?

Phone messages

Hi, Yoko. This is Tim. I'm really sorry I can't come to your party.

an apology

Rika. Would you like to come to my place for dinner on Friday?

an invitation

Hiro, don't forget to pick up the tickets.

a reminder

Could I please speak to Amy?

a request

She's not here. Can I take a message?

an offer

Why don't you call her at work?

a suggestion

---

1   Speaking   Class CD1 Track 34

A   Listen and look at the pictures. Then practice with a partner.

> A: *What's the message about?*
> B: *It's an apology for not going to a party.*

B   Pretend to call your partner's answering machine and leave a message.

Hello, Jean. This is Ari. Please call me on my cell phone: 917-555-9655.

---

2   Listening   Class CD1 Track 35

People are leaving phone messages. What kind of message does each person leave? Listen and check (✓) the correct answer.

1. **a.** ☐ an invitation to a movie
   b. ☐ an apology for missing a movie
   c. ☐ a suggestion for a movie to see

2. **a.** ☐ a request to borrow a camera
   b. ☐ a reminder about a camera
   c. ☐ an offer to lend a camera

3. **a.** ☐ an offer to change a meeting time
   b. ☐ a request to change a meeting time
   c. ☐ a reminder about a meeting time

4. **a.** ☐ an apology for missing a basketball game
   b. ☐ a suggestion about a basketball game
   c. ☐ an offer about a basketball game

Listen. Then listen again and repeat.

Can you please **take** a message?	Sure. What's the message?
Will you **give** her my cell phone number, please?	No problem. What's the number?
Could you please **ask** him to call me back?	Yes, certainly.
Would you **tell** her I called, please?	I'll be glad to.

> **Memo**
>
> You can use *please* in the middle or at the end of a polite request:
>
> Can you *please* take a message?
>
> Can you take a message, *please*?

4 **Conversation** Class CD1 Track 37

A *Pair work.* Listen to the conversation. Then practice with a partner.

A: Hello.

B: Hi, Junko. It's Carl. Could I please speak to Emma?

A: Oh, hi, Carl. I'm afraid Emma isn't home right now.

B: What time do you expect her to be back?

A: She'll be home by five. Would you like to leave a message?

B: Yeah, I would. Would you please tell her I called? And could you ask her to call me back on my cell phone?

A: Sure. Does she have your cell phone number?

B: I think so, but will you give her my number anyway, just in case she doesn't have it?

A: No problem. What's the number?

B: It's 617-555-6424.

A: That's 617-555-6424. Right?

B: That's right. Thanks a lot, Junko.

B *Pair work.* Practice the conversation again. Use different names and information.

Student A looks at this page. Student B looks at page 74.

Pair work. Look at the conversations below. You have directions for part A of the conversations, and your partner has directions for part B. Role-play the conversations. Use *can, will, could,* and *would* in requests.

Conversation 1

A: Answer the phone.
B: ....
A: Say Erin is not there. Ask if you can take a message.
B: ....
A: Say you'll give Erin the message.
B: ....

Conversation 2

B: ....
A: Ask to speak to Yoji Yamada.
B: ....
A: Say yes. Ask B to tell Yoji he left his cell phone in your car. Ask B to tell Yoji you'll give him the phone tomorrow.
B: ....
A: Give your name and phone number.
B: ....
A: Thank B, and end the call.

Conversation 3

A: Answer the phone.
B: ....
A: Say Tasha is at work right now.
B: ....
A: Say you'll give Tasha the message.
B: ....
A: Say yes. Ask for the number.
B: ....
A: End the call.

Extra

Think of an unusual request. Call your partner and make your request. Role-play the conversation. Take turns calling and making your requests.
A: *Hi, Miko. This is Frank.*
B: *Oh, hi, Frank. How are you?*
A: *I'm fine, thanks. I'm calling to ask something.*
B: *Sure, what is it?*
A: *Well, could you please...?*

Favors and requests

You can pay me back tomorrow.

lend someone money

give someone a ride

pick up something (at a store)

save a seat for someone

give someone directions

wait for someone

6 Speaking
Class CD1
Track 38

A Listen and look at the pictures. Then practice with a partner.

A: What is he doing?
B: He's lending someone money.

B Have you done any of the things in the pictures? Tell your partner.

I lent my brother money last week.

7 Listening
Class CD1
Track 39

A People are asking for favors. What do they ask people to do? Listen and number the items from 1 to 6.

_____ lend them something   _____ give them a ride   _____ pick up something at a store
_____ save a seat for them   _____ wait for them   _____ give them directions

B Listen again. Does the person agree to do the favor? Check (✓) Yes or No.

1. ❏ Yes   3. ❏ Yes   5. ❏ Yes
    ❏ No   ❏ No   ❏ No

2. ❏ Yes   4. ❏ Yes   6. ❏ Yes
    ❏ No   ❏ No   ❏ No

8 Grammar: *Requests with* Would you mind...?

A Listen. Then listen again and repeat.

Would you mind + gerund	***Would you mind if*** + the simple past
Would you mind lending me some money?	**Would you mind if** I **waited** for her?
Not at all. How much do you need?	Of course not. She'll be here soon.
Would you mind not calling me so late?	**Would you mind if** I **didn't go** with you?
Oh, I'm sorry. I won't do it again.	No problem. I'll go alone.

B *Pair work.* Take turns making requests. Use the ideas below or your own ideas. Partners respond.

lend you his/her cell phone
turn off the air conditioner

turn on the light
open the window

close the door
tell you the time

Would you mind lending me your cell phone?

Not at all. Here it is.

9 Conversation

A *Pair work.* Listen to the conversation. Then practice with a partner.

A: Oh, Nancy. Are you working late again tonight?

B: Yes, I am.

A: Me, too. I'm going downstairs to pick up something to eat. Do you want to come with me?

B: Would you mind if I didn't go with you? I have a few calls to make.

A: No problem. Can I get anything for you downstairs?

B: Oh, yes! Would you mind picking up a sandwich for me?

A: Not at all. What kind do you want?

B: Chicken salad. And could you get me a coffee, too?

A: Sure! I'll be back in a few minutes.

B: Thanks, Neil.

B *Pair work.* Practice the conversation again. Use different names and information.

A Read about the situations below. Pretend you are in each situation. Think about how to make each request.

You're with a friend at the post office. You need a pen to fill out a form. Your friend has a pen. What would you say?

You're going on vacation. Your camera is broken. Your friend has an old camera she probably isn't using. What would you say to your friend?

You're in a park. You see a stranger with a beautiful dog. You want to pet the dog. What would you say to the stranger?

You're in a clothing store. You want to see if a sweater fits before you buy it. What would you say to the salesperson?

You're with a friend watching a football game. Your friend has a pair of binoculars. You do not. You want to borrow them for a moment. What would you say?

You're buying an MP3 player in an electronics store. You want to know if you can pay by credit card. What would you say to the salesperson?

You're on vacation with a friend and are climbing a mountain. You're exhausted and want to stop for a moment. What would you say?

You're a passenger in a taxi. You think the driver is driving too fast. What would you say to the driver?

You're getting on a bus. A person in the bus line is pushing in front of you. What would you say to that person?

You're on a tour bus with a good friend. After a few days you want to change seats. What would you say to your friend?

B *Pair work.* Choose a situation from above and make an appropriate request. Partners respond. Take turns.

Wishes

meet more people

have more money

move to a new apartment

enjoy life more

know how to dance

be taller

1 Speaking

 Class CD1
Track 42

A Listen and look at the pictures. Then practice with a partner.

A: What does she wish?
B: She wishes she could meet more people.

B What do you wish? Tell your partner.

I wish I...

2 Listening

 Class CD1
Track 43

People are talking about wishes. What does each person wish?
Listen and write the letter of the correct answer.

1. Corey wishes he ___   **a.** could meet more people.
2. Dana wishes she ___   **b.** had more money.
3. Koji wishes he ___   **c.** had a bigger apartment.
4. Leya wishes she ___   **d.** knew how to dance.
5. Chet wishes he ___   **e.** enjoyed life more.
6. Tracy wishes she ___   **f.** were taller.

3 Grammar: *Verb forms after* wish

Listen. Then listen again and repeat.

Wishes about the present	
I'm poor.	I wish I **were** rich.
It's **raining**.	I wish it **weren't raining**.
I **can't drive**.	I wish I **could drive**.
I **don't have** a car.	I wish I **had** a car.
I **don't know** her.	I wish I **knew** her.
Wishes about the future	
He **won't tell** me.	I wish he **would tell** me.
He **can't go** tomorrow.	I wish he **could go** tomorrow.
She **isn't going to be** there.	I wish she **were going to be** there.

Memo
am/is/are → were
can → could
have → had
know → knew
will → would

4 Conversation

A *Pair work.* Listen to the conversation. Then practice with a partner.

A: Hello?

B: Hi, Charlie! It's me, Jung-soo. How are you?

A: Uh, OK. But this weather's really depressing.
I wish it would stop raining.

B: Don't worry. It'll stop soon.

A: I hope you're right. What are you doing tonight?
Do you want to go to a movie?

B: Oh, I wish I could go, but I can't. I have to study
for a test.

A: Oh, that's too bad. I wish you didn't have to study.

B: Me, too. Maybe we can see a movie on the
weekend.

A: Good idea. Let's do that.

B *Pair work.* Practice the conversation again. Use your
imagination and change the information.

Extra

Use the ideas below to make sentences with *wish*. Explain to your
partner why you are making each wish. Take turns.

play a musical instrument	*be a famous movie star*
have your own apartment	*have more money*
live somewhere different	*be in love*

I wish I could play the drums. It would be fun to play in a band.

A Look at the questions. Which ones would you like to answer? In your mind, think about how you would answer them.

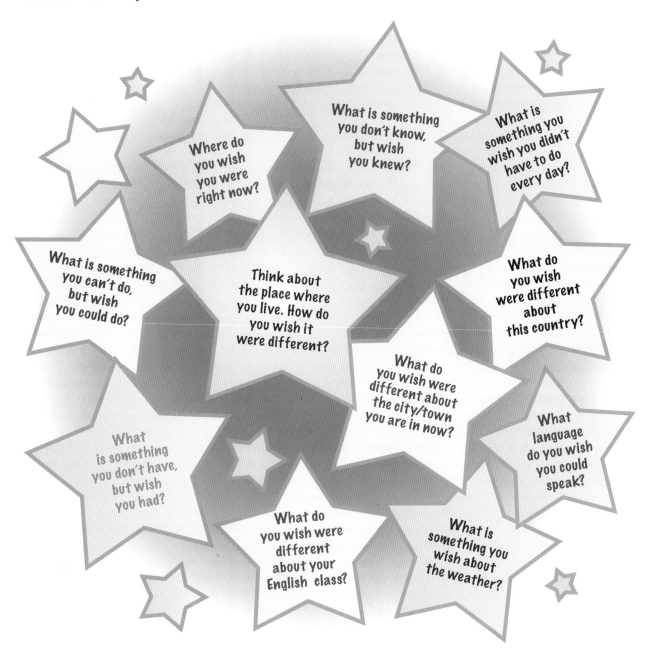

Where do you wish you were right now?

What is something you don't know, but wish you knew?

What is something you wish you didn't have to do every day?

What is something you can't do, but wish you could do?

Think about the place where you live. How do you wish it were different?

What do you wish were different about this country?

What do you wish were different about the city/town you are in now?

What is something you don't have, but wish you had?

What language do you wish you could speak?

What do you wish were different about your English class?

What is something you wish about the weather?

B *Pair work.* Point to a question and answer it. Partners ask for more information. Take turns.

> A: (Pointing to the question "Where do you wish you were right now?")
>   I wish I were at home right now.
> B: Really? Why?
> A: Because I'm tired, and I want to go to bed.

Opinions

tattoos

credit cards

household pets

TV commercials

school uniforms

fast food

6 Speaking
Class CD1 Track 46

A Listen and look at the pictures. Then practice with a partner.

A: What are they?
B: They're tattoos.

B Which things are you *for*? Which things are you *against*? Tell your partner.

> I'm *for* tattoos.
> I'm against…

7 Listening
Class CD1 Track 47

A People are giving opinions. Which topic are they talking about? Listen and number the topics from 1 to 6.

____ tattoos   ____ credit cards   ____ household pets
____ TV commercials   ____ school uniforms   ____ fast food

B Listen again. Do the people agree about the topic? Check (✓) the correct answer.

1. ❑ Agree   3. ❑ Agree   5. ❑ Agree
    ❑ Don't agree   ❑ Don't agree   ❑ Don't agree

2. ❑ Agree   4. ❑ Agree   6. ❑ Agree
    ❑ Don't agree   ❑ Don't agree   ❑ Don't agree

A Listen. Then listen again and repeat.

With adjectives	With nouns
That movie is **too** violent for children.	That movie has **too much** violence.
Bobby is**n't** old **enough** to see that movie.	There are **too many** TV commercials.
	There are**n't enough** programs for children.

Memo

Use *too many* with count nouns.
Use *too much* with non-count nouns.

B *Pair work.* Take turns giving opinions with *too* or *enough*. Use the ideas below or your own ideas.

air travel   hip-hop music
the Internet   professional wrestling

 I think air travel is too expensive.

9 **Conversation** Class CD1 Track 49

A *Pair work.* Listen to the conversation. Then practice with a partner.

A: So how do you like living in the city?
B: I love it! There are enough museums and art galleries to keep me happy for years! It's too bad I don't have enough time to enjoy them.
A: Why not?
B: I'm too busy at the office. There are too many projects and not enough people to work on them.
A: That's too bad.
B: I'm too busy to meet new people or make friends. I wish I had more time to go out.
A: I'm sure things will get better soon.

B *Pair work.* Practice the conversation again. Give your own opinions about living in your city or town.

A Think about each topic below. For each one, write an opinion about what is sufficient (*enough*), insufficient (*not enough*), or excessive (*too many/much*) in some place you know.

Public transportation:

Public transportation in this city is too expensive.

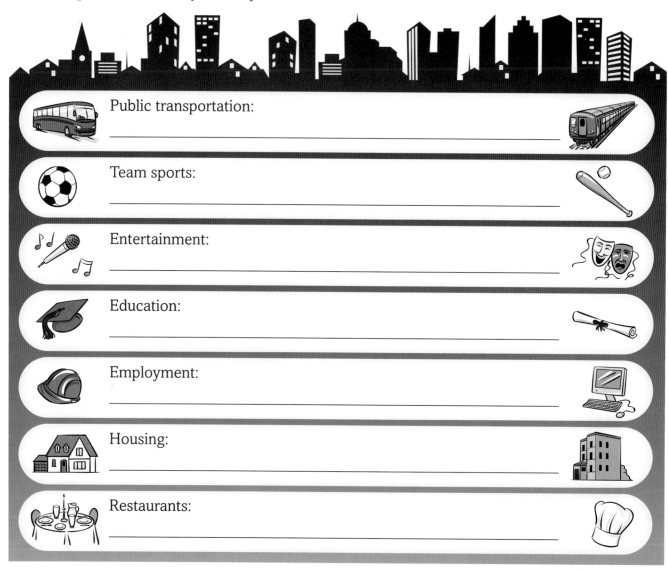

Public transportation:
_____

Team sports:
_____

Entertainment:
_____

Education:
_____

Employment:
_____

Housing:
_____

Restaurants:
_____

B *Pair work.* Take turns reading your opinions to your partner. Partners say whether they agree or disagree and give their own opinions.

    A: Public transportation in this city is too expensive.
    B: You're right about that. And there aren't enough buses.

OR

Really? I think it's cheap enough, but the subway is too crowded.

Helpful Language
....
- I totally agree.
- You're right about that.
- That's true, but...
- Really? I think...

Customs

eating bread

bowing

tipping

shaking hands

using chopsticks

removing shoes

1 Speaking
Class CD2
Track 2

A Listen and look at the pictures. Then practice with a partner.

A: What are they doing?
B: They're eating bread.

B Where do you think each custom is typical? Tell your partner.

> **Eating bread with a meal is typical in France.**

2 Listening
Class CD2
Track 3

People are giving advice about customs. Which custom is each person talking about? Listen and number the customs from 1 to 6.

____ removing shoes   ____ eating bread   ____ shaking hands

____ using chopsticks   ____ bowing   ____ tipping

Listen. Then listen again and repeat.

It + infinitive	Gerunds as subjects
It's unnecessary **to tip** taxi drivers in Vietnam.	**Tipping** taxi drivers is unnecessary in Vietnam.
It's customary **to eat** with chopsticks in Taiwan.	**Eating** with chopsticks is customary in Taiwan.
It's common **to serve** dinner after 9:00 P.M. in Spain.	**Serving** dinner after 9:00 P.M. is common in Spain.
It's impolite **to whistle** in India.	**Whistling** is impolite in India.

4 **Conversation** Class CD2
Track 5

A *Pair work.* Listen to the conversation. Then practice with a partner.

A: Guess what, Nikom! I'm going to Thailand next month.

B: Wow! That's great. Maybe you can visit my family while you're there.

A: That would be very nice, but I'll need some advice about Thai customs. I've never been there before.

B: Well, it's important to smile a lot in Thailand. Smiling is the easiest way to say thank you.

A: That's easy to remember. What about shoes? Do I have to take them off when I enter someone's home?

B: Yes, removing your shoes is customary.

A: Anything else?

B: Yes, one very important thing. Touching or patting a person's head is impolite.

B *Pair work.* Practice the conversation again. Use real names and give true information about a country you know.

> **Extra**
>
> Make sentences about customs in your country. Use the gerund or infinitive form of these verbs. Read your sentences to your partner. Take turns.
>
> *bring a gift* *talk loudly* *eat with your fingers*
> *ask personal questions* *use first names* *point at someone*
> *Bringing a gift to a birthday party is customary in...*

Student A looks at this page. Student B looks at page 75.

A *Pair work.* Look at the quiz below. You and your partner each have a different version of the quiz. Read each statement to your partner. Your partner says whether the statement is true or false. Check (✓) the answer your partner thinks is correct for each statement.

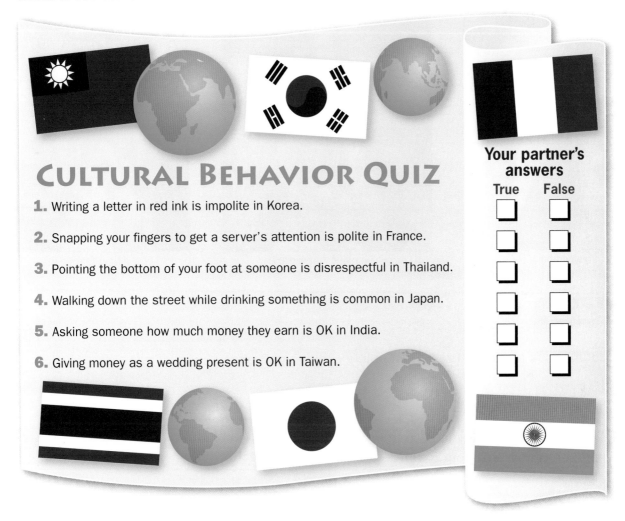

CULTURAL BEHAVIOR QUIZ

1. Writing a letter in red ink is impolite in Korea.

2. Snapping your fingers to get a server's attention is polite in France.

3. Pointing the bottom of your foot at someone is disrespectful in Thailand.

4. Walking down the street while drinking something is common in Japan.

5. Asking someone how much money they earn is OK in India.

6. Giving money as a wedding present is OK in Taiwan.

Your partner's answers

True   False

B *Pair work.* Now your partner will read six statements to you. Say whether you think each statement is true or false.

C *Pair work.* Here are the correct answers to the statements above: 1T, 2F, 3T, 4F, 5F, 6T. Tell your partner the correct answer for each statement. Take turns.

D *Group work.* Get together with another pair. Ask and answer these questions:

Which of these behaviors are OK to do in your country?
Which behaviors are rude?
Which ones have you done?
Which ones have you seen or heard other people do?

Events and celebrations

a birthday party

a graduation

a dinner party

a wedding

a wedding anniversary

a New Year's party

6   Speaking

 Class CD2 Track 6

A   Listen and look at the pictures. Then practice with a partner.

A: What kind of event is this?
B: It's a birthday party.

B   What special events have you been to or celebrated recently? Tell your partner.

> I went to a birthday party last week.

7   Listening

 Class CD2 Track 7

A   Listen to people talking about special days and events. What events are they talking about? Listen and number the events from 1 to 6.

____ a wedding   ____ a graduation   ____ a dinner party
____ a birthday party   ____ an anniversary   ____ a New Year's party

B   Listen again. What do the people say about each event? Circle the correct answer.

1. There <u>were / weren't</u> a lot of people there.

2. The party was at <u>a restaurant / an apartment</u>.

3. Her parents <u>were / weren't</u> there.

4. He <u>took / didn't take</u> a lot of pictures.

5. It happened last <u>week / month</u>.

6. He <u>bought / didn't buy</u> a present.

A Listen. Then listen again and repeat.

> **Before** a dinner party, people usually clean the house and shop for food.
> People usually clean the house and shop for food **before** a dinner party.
>
> **When** people arrive at a dinner party, they often give the host a small gift of food or flowers.
> People often give the host a small gift of food or flowers **when** they arrive at a dinner party.
>
> **After** a dinner party, people usually call to thank the host and say they had a good time.
> People usually call to thank the host and say they had a good time **after** a dinner party.

Memo
A comma (,) is used when the time clause comes first in a sentence.

B *Pair work.* Ask and answer questions with *before*, *when*, and *after*.

> **What do you usually do before you come to English class?**

> **Before I come to class, I usually eat lunch.**

A *Pair work.* Listen to the conversation. Then practice with a partner.

A: Hi, Jennie! What are you reading?

B: An article about wedding customs around the world. Did you know that in Chile couples exchange wedding rings *before* they get married?

A: They don't exchange them at the wedding?

B: No, they exchange rings when they get engaged. And they wear them on their right hands until they get married. After they get married, they wear the rings on their left hands.

A: Interesting. Any other unusual customs?

B: Yeah, here's one. In Sweden, before a bride goes to the church to be married, her parents put two coins in her shoes.

A: Why do they do that?

B: So the bride will always have money!

B *Pair work.* Practice the conversation again. Use real names and talk about wedding customs you know.

Group activity. Work in a group of three or four. Take turns. Follow these instructions.

1. Choose a marker (an eraser, a coin, or a small piece of paper with your initials) and place it on START.

2. Toss a coin and move your marker one or two spaces. "Heads" means one space. "Tails" means two spaces.

3. When you land on a space, imagine you are in the situation described in the space. Ask your group for advice. Group members take turns giving advice using *Before/When/After you …* in their sentences.

> A: *I'm taking an important exam next week. Yu-lin, what's your advice?*
> B: *Before you take an exam, study hard.*
> A: *Thanks. What about you, Wei-de? What's your advice?*
> C: *When you take an exam, try to relax.*

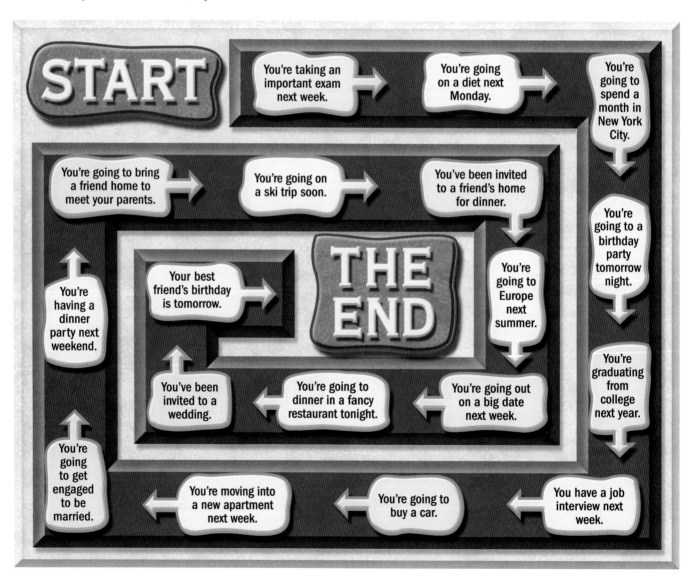

Jobs

graphic artist

sports instructor

dancer

mechanic

police officer

hairdresser

reporter

photographer

manager

firefighter

surgeon

cashier

1 Speaking
 Class CD2
Track 10

A Listen and look at the pictures. Then practice with a partner.

A: What kind of work does she do?
B: She's a graphic artist.

B What job would you like to have? Tell your partner.

> **I'd like to be a photographer.**

2 Listening
 Class CD2
Track 11

People are talking about their jobs. What job does each person have?
Listen and check (✓) the correct answer.

1. **a.** ☐ surgeon
   b. ☑ police officer

2. **a.** ☐ manager
   b. ☐ photographer

3. **a.** ☐ reporter
   b. ☐ graphic artist

4. **a.** ☐ cashier
   b. ☐ hairdresser

5. **a.** ☐ mechanic
   b. ☐ firefighter

6. **a.** ☐ dancer
   b. ☐ sports instructor

Listen. Then listen again and repeat.

How long have you **worked** here?		
I've worked here **since** I graduated.	**I've worked** here **for** a few years.	
How long has he **had** that job?		
He's had that job **since** 1997.	**He's had** that job **for** a long time.	
How long have they **been** here?		
They've been here **since** ten o'clock.	**They've been** here **for** two hours.	

Memo

Use *since* to say when something started.

Use *for* to say how long something has lasted.

4   **Conversation**   Class CD2 Track 13

A   *Pair work.* Listen to the conversation. Then practice with a partner.

A: Hello, Ms. Suzuki. How are you?

B: I'm fine, thank you. I'm here to apply for the position as a graphic artist. I have lots of experience.

A: How long have you worked as a graphic artist?

B: I've worked as a graphic artist for five years. I've worked with the Green Agency since 2000.

A: Do you have experience designing websites?

B: Yes, I do. I've designed websites since I was in high school. That's how I got my job with the Green Agency. They saw one of my websites and offered me a job.

A: I'll look at your resumé, and I'll call you next week. We've had this job opening for a long time now. I hope you're right for the job.

B: Me, too. Thank you so much for your time.

B   *Pair work.* Practice the conversation again. Pretend you are at a job interview. Use your imagination. Take turns being the employer.

Extra

Find out at least three things about your partner. Ask questions with *how long*. Use the verbs below. Take turns.

live in	own	study	have	know (someone)

A: *How long have you lived in Seoul?*

B: *I've lived in Seoul since I was five years old.*

5 Communication task: A job interview

A Write a resumé. Use the resumé below as a model. You can use real or imaginary information.

Mariko Kotoku 44 Rosehill Street, Los Angeles, CA 90046
(555) 555-1010

Education:

Certificate in Web Design (Internet Institute); 2003

MA in Arts Education (UCLA); 2002

Employment:

Art teacher (Central High School); 2002–Present

Part-time arts and crafts teacher (YMCA); 1999–Present

Skills:

Speak Japanese and Spanish

Awards:

Teacher of the Year Award; 2005

First Prize in California Student Art Show; 2001

Memberships:

Member of American Teachers Association (ATA); 2001–Present

B *Pair work.* Give your resumé to a partner. Then role-play a job interview. Answer your partner's questions about your career. Use your imagination to answer questions you don't have definite answers for. Take turns being the interviewer and the candidate.

Helpful Language

- What kind of job are you looking for?
- How long have you been/had/worked/lived in/studied...?
- What did you like most about your last job?
- When/Why did you...?

use the Internet

supervise people

attend meetings

write reports

answer questions

take business trips

6 Speaking

Class CD2
Track 14

A Listen and look at the pictures. Then practice with a partner.

A: Does he use the Internet at work?
B: Yes, he does.

B Which things do you do or hope to do at work? Which things are you good at doing? Tell your partner.

> I hope to take business trips. I'm good at using the Internet.

7 Listening

Class CD2
Track 15

A People are talking about their jobs. What do they do at work? Listen and check (✓) the correct answers. There is more than one answer for each item.

	Uses the Internet	Supervises people	Attends meetings	Writes reports	Answers questions	Takes business trips
1.	❑	❑	❑	❑	❑	❑
2.	❑	❑	❑	❑	❑	❑
3.	❑	❑	❑	❑	❑	❑
4.	❑	❑	❑	❑	❑	❑

B Listen again. Do the people like or dislike their jobs? Check (✓) Yes or No.

1. ❑ Yes ❑ No   2. ❑ Yes ❑ No   3. ❑ Yes ❑ No   4. ❑ Yes ❑ No

A Listen. Then listen again and repeat.

Verb + infinitive	Verb or phrase + gerund
She **wants to supervise** people.	He **enjoys using** the Internet.
She **needs to attend** meetings.	He's **good at writing** reports.
She **plans to get** a new job.	He's **tired of taking** business trips.

Memo

Followed by infinitive
need, plan, expect, want, hope

Followed by gerund
enjoy, dislike, avoid, feel like, regret,
be afraid of,
be good at,
be interested in,
be tired of,
be nervous about

B *Pair work.* Ask and answer questions with your partner. Use the verbs and phrases in the Memo.

> **Is there anything you need to do today?**

> **Yes. I need to check my e-mail.**

9 **Conversation** Class CD2 Track 17

A *Pair work.* Listen to the conversation. Then practice with a partner.

A: What are you planning to do after you graduate? What kind of work do you want to do?

B: Well, I'm interested in business.

A: What kind of business?

B: The music business.

A: That's interesting. Are you good at working with people?

B: I think I am. I'd like to work with musicians. I'm interested in managing them and helping them become famous. What about you? What are you interested in?

A: I'm really interested in travel. I also like to read and learn about new places.

B: Have you thought about going into the travel business? You could be a tour guide or something like that.

B *Pair work.* Practice the conversation again. Use real names and give true information about yourself.

A Look at the topics below. Which ones do you want to talk about?
Think about what you can say about each topic.

Something you enjoy
doing on weekends

Something you are
good at doing

Something you need
to do today

Something you like
to do alone

Something you plan
to do after class

Something you usually
avoid doing

Something you are
afraid of doing

Something you
are tired of doing

Something you
hate to do

Something you prefer
to do with friends

Something you feel like
doing right now

Something you expect
to do tomorrow

B *Group work.* Choose a topic. Say one or two sentences about it. Members
of the group ask follow-up questions to get more information. Take turns.

A: *I enjoy listening to music on weekends. I like to listen to jazz.*
B: *Do you ever go to jazz clubs?*
A: *Yes, I do.*
C: *What jazz clubs do you go to?*
A: *I usually go to…*
D: *Who's your favorite jazz musician?*
A: *My favorite jazz musician is…*

Recent activities

train for a race

daydream

take driving lessons

learn how to draw

take a cooking course

spend time at a theme park

look for a job

get a lot of sleep

1 Speaking
Class CD2
Track 18

A Listen and look at the pictures. Then practice with a partner.

A: What has he been doing lately?
B: He's been training for a race.

B What have you been doing lately? Tell your partner.

> I've been looking for a job. I…

2 Listening
Class CD2
Track 19

People are talking about recent activities. What has each person been doing? Listen and check (✓) the correct answer.

1. **a.** ❑ daydreaming
   b. ❑ spending time at a theme park
   c. ❑ training for a race

2. **a.** ❑ taking a cooking course
   b. ❑ looking for a job
   c. ❑ training for a race

3. **a.** ❑ spending time at a theme park
   b. ❑ getting a lot of sleep
   c. ❑ taking driving lessons

4. **a.** ❑ learning how to draw
   b. ❑ taking driving lessons
   c. ❑ taking a cooking course

3 Grammar: *The present perfect continuous*

Listen. Then listen again and repeat.

What **have** you **been doing** lately?	I**'ve been writing** a paper.
How long **have** you **been writing** it?	I**'ve been writing** it for two days.
Have you **been getting** a lot of sleep?	No, I **haven't been getting** a lot of sleep.

Memo

Use the present perfect continuous to talk about actions that started in the past and continue into the present.

4 Conversation

 Class CD2
Track 21

A *Pair work.* Listen to the conversation. Then practice with a partner.

A: Hey, Carla! I haven't seen you for ages. What have you been up to lately?

B: Not much, really. I've been studying a lot. I have a paper due next week. How about you? What have you been doing?

A: I've been learning how to draw. I go to class three times a week.

B: No kidding! How long have you been doing that?

A: A couple of months.

B: How's your sister doing? I haven't seen her for a long time.

A: My sister Betty? She's fine. She's been looking for a better job since June.

B: Good for her! I hope she finds something she really likes. Well, it's been nice talking to you.

A: Good luck on your paper!

B: Thanks.

B *Pair work.* Practice the conversation again. Use your imagination and change the information.

Extra

Practice the conversation again. Use some of the expressions in the Helpful Language note.

Helpful Language

Greeting people:
- How have you been?
- How's everything?
- How's it going?

Ending a conversation:
- It's been great talking to you.
- It's been nice seeing you again.
- Hope to see you again soon.

Pair work. Look at the pictures. Take turns describing the people in each picture. What are they doing? Where are they doing it? How long have they been doing it? Why have they been doing it? Use your imagination. Say as much as you can about each person.

1. Mari is outside a movie theater. She's waiting for her boyfriend. She's been waiting since…

1.

2.

3.

4.

5.

6.

Extra

With a partner ask and answer questions about the people in the pictures. Use *who, what, where, why, how many,* and *how long* in your questions.

A: *Who's been waiting for someone?*
B: *Mari has.*
A: *How long has she been waiting?*
B: *She's been waiting for…*

Leisure activities

go (horseback) riding

hang out with friends

practice martial arts

build a website

play racquetball

go to concerts

6 Speaking
Class CD2
Track 22

A Listen and look at the pictures. Then practice with a partner.

A: What have they been doing?
B: They've been going horseback riding.

B Which activities do you enjoy doing? Tell your partner.

> I enjoy hanging out with friends. I enjoy…

7 Listening
Class CD2
Track 23

A People are talking about leisure activities. Which activities are they talking about?
Listen and number the activities from 1 to 6.

____ horseback riding   ____ hanging out   ____ practicing martial arts
____ building a website   ____ playing racquetball   ____ going to concerts

B Listen again. Check (✓) the best response.

1. **a.** ❏ I'm not very good at it.
   b. ❏ For about a year.

2. **a.** ❏ Yeah. I'd like to do that.
   b. ❏ How long have you been doing that?

3. **a.** ❏ I've had three.
   b. ❏ Since I was 15.

4. **a.** ❏ I've had four.
   b. ❏ For eight years.

5. **a.** ❏ No, not yet.
   b. ❏ I've done it once.

6. **a.** ❏ Since he came home.
   b. ❏ Every weekend.

A Listen. Then listen again and repeat.

The present perfect continuous	The present perfect
What **have** you **been doing** lately? I've **been building** websites.	How many websites **have** you **built**? I've **built** three sites.
What **has** he **been doing** lately? He's **been going** to concerts a lot.	How many times **has** he **gone** to a concert this week? He's **gone** to a concert twice this week.
What **has** she **been doing** lately? She's **been playing** racquetball.	How many games **has** she **played**? She's **played** four games.

Memo

• Use the present perfect continuous to talk about continuing situations:
I've been playing racquetball a lot lately.

• Use the present perfect to talk about things that are completed:
I've played racquetball three times this week.

B *Pair work.* Tell your partner what you have been doing lately. Use the present perfect continuous. Partners ask follow-up questions with the present perfect.

> I've been drinking a lot of coffee.

> How many cups of coffee have you had today?

9 **Conversation** Class CD2 Track 25

A *Pair work.* Listen to the conversation. Then practice with a partner.

A: Hi, Mimi!

B: Oh, hi, Hannah! How have you been?

A: Just fine. How about you? I haven't seen you for a while. What have you been doing? Anything interesting?

B: Well, I've been going horseback riding.

A: Really? I didn't know that. Have you been taking lessons?

B: Yes. At the BTA Stables. I've already taken eight lessons.

A: No kidding! How are you doing?

B: Great! I think I'm becoming a really good rider.

B *Pair work.* Practice the conversation again. Use your imagination and change the information. Take turns being A and B.

Extra

Take turns talking about things your friends or members of your family have been doing lately. Partners ask questions to find out more information.

A: *My brother has been working very hard lately.*

B: *Where has he been working?*

A: *He's been working at…*

A What has your partner been doing lately? Check (✓) your guesses.

Has your partner...	My guesses		My partner's answers	
	YES	NO	YES	NO
1 seen any good movies lately?	○	○	○	○
2 read any good books lately?	○	○	○	○
3 been learning to drive?	○	○	○	○
4 been playing basketball?	○	○	○	○
5 been taking cooking lessons?	○	○	○	○
6 been looking for a job?	○	○	○	○
7 been sleeping a lot?	○	○	○	○
8 been hanging out with friends?	○	○	○	○
9 been saving money?	○	○	○	○
10 gone shopping this week?	○	○	○	○
11 taken a lot of photos recently?	○	○	○	○
12 been to any concerts this month?	○	○	○	○

B *Pair work.* Ask your partner questions to check your answers. Partners ask questions with *what, where, how long, how many,* or *how much* to find out more information.

A: *Have you seen any good movies lately?*
B: *Yes, I have.*
A: *Really? Which ones have you seen?*
B: *I've seen…*

C *Class activity.* Take turns. Tell the class what your partner has been doing lately.

Helpful Language
- What have you…?
- Where have you…?
- How long have you…?
- How many/much have you…?

mustache

muscular

wavy hair

bald

beard

scruffy

lazy

neat

confident

studious

I Speaking   Class CD2 Track 26

A Listen and look at the pictures. Then practice with a partner.

A: Does he have a mustache?
B: Yes, he does.

B Describe yourself to your partner.

> I have short, straight hair, and I'm…

2 Listening   Class CD2 Track 27

People are describing other people. How do they describe them? Listen and check (✓)
the correct answers. There is more than one answer for each item.

1. The new manager	❏ bald	❏ wavy hair	❏ mustache	❏ muscular
2. Jay's brother	❏ muscular	❏ neat	❏ beard	❏ mustache
3. Alison	❏ scruffy	❏ confident	❏ studious	❏ neat
4. The tour guide	❏ neat	❏ scruffy	❏ confident	❏ lazy

Listen. Then listen again and repeat.

Did you **use to be** neat?	Yes, **I did. I used to be** neat. **I didn't use to be** so messy.
Did you **use to have** a mustache?	No, **I didn't. I didn't use to have** a mustache. **I used to have** a beard.
How **did** you **use to go** to school?	**I used to ride** a bike to school, but now I take the subway.

Memo

- Use *used to* to talk about things that were true in the past but are not true in the present:
  I *used to* get up early, but now I get up late.
- Use *used to* for affirmative statements.
- Use *use to* for questions and negative statements.

A *Pair work.* Listen to the conversation. Then practice with a partner.

A: Is that Kim Fisher? She looks so different! I think it's her hair.

B: Yeah, it's her. I was talking to her a few minutes ago. She used to have really long hair. Look how short it is now! Doesn't she look great?

A: Yeah, she does. Remember how she used to be kind of scruffy? How did she get to be so neat?

B: I don't know, but she really has changed a lot. And by the way, so have you. You didn't use to be so confident!

A: I know. I used to be shy.

B *Pair work.* Practice the conversation again. Use your imagination and change the information.

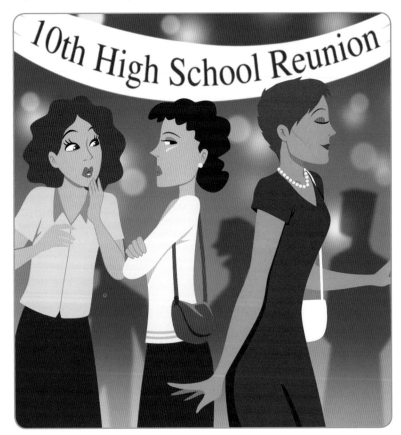

Extra

Talk about your family or other people you know. Say how they have changed. Your partner asks questions.
A: *My brother used to live in Osaka. Now he lives in Los Angeles.*
B: *Why did he move to Los Angeles?*
A: *He went there to go to film school.*

A   Think about how you and your life used to be five years ago. Make notes in the chart about things that are different.

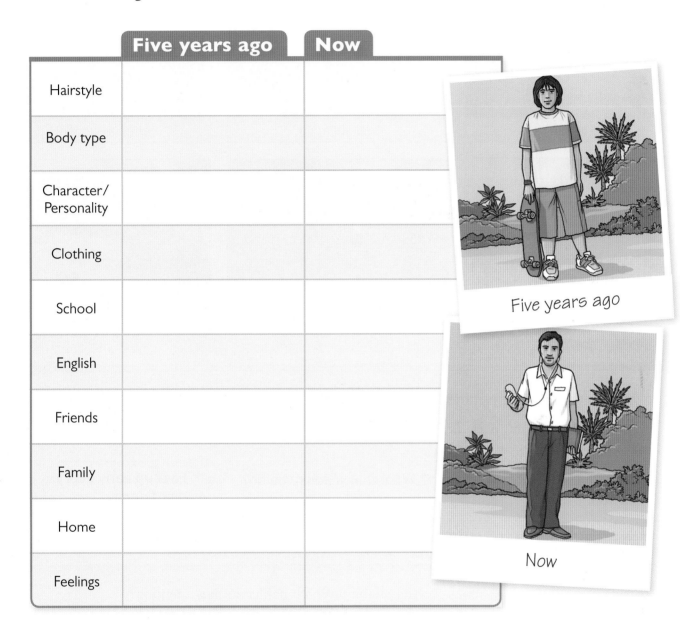

	Five years ago	Now
Hairstyle		
Body type		
Character/ Personality		
Clothing		
School		
English		
Friends		
Family		
Home		
Feelings		

Five years ago

Now

B   *Pair work.* Take turns describing how you have changed in the past five years. Partners ask questions to find out more information.

A: *I used to have long hair, but now my hair is short.*
B: *When did you cut your hair?*
A: *Two years ago.*
B: *Why did you cut it?*
A: *I cut it because…*

Everyday habits

get up early

use an alarm clock

have a big breakfast

read the newspaper

ride a bike to school

go to bed late

6 Speaking
Class CD2
Track 30

A Listen and look at the pictures. Then practice with a partner.

> A: Does he get up early every day?
> B: Yes, he does.

B What things do you do every day? What things don't you do? Tell your partner.

> **I get up early every day. I don't…**

7 Listening
Class CD2
Track 31

A Listen to people talking about everyday habits. Which habits do they mention? Listen and number them from 1 to 6.

| _____ having a big breakfast | _____ going to bed late | _____ using an alarm clock |
| _____ getting up early | _____ riding a bike | _____ reading the newspaper |

B Listen again. How often does each person do the habit? Check (✓) the correct answer.

1. **a.** ☐ almost always
   b. ☐ hardly ever

2. **a.** ☐ twice a week
   b. ☐ every day

3. **a.** ☐ almost every day
   b. ☐ once in a while

4. **a.** ☐ often
   b. ☐ rarely

5. **a.** ☐ once a week
   b. ☐ almost never

6. **a.** ☐ never
   b. ☐ all the time

8 Grammar: *The simple past with* how long

Class CD2
Track 32

A Listen. Then listen again and repeat.

How long did you **live** in Osaka?	I **lived** there for 15 years.
How long were you a teacher?	I **was** a teacher from 1999 to 2004.
How long did you **stay** there?	I **stayed** there until 2005.

Memo
- Use *how long* with the simple past to ask about actions or situations that have ended.
- Use *how long* with the present perfect or present perfect continuous to ask about actions or situations that continue in the present.

B *Pair work.* Ask your partner questions about the past. Use *how long*. Take turns.

How long were you in film school?

(I was in film school) for two years.

9 Conversation
Class CD2
Track 33

A *Pair work.* Listen to the conversation. Then practice with a partner.

A: Could you tell me something about your early life?
B: Well, when I was little, I used to get up early and ride my bike to school every day.
A: Where did you grow up?
B: I grew up in Texas.
A: How long did you live there?
B: I was there for 18 years. I lived there until I graduated from high school.
A: Did you always want to be an actor?
B: Oh, yeah. When I was young, I used to dream about being an actor. After I graduated from high school, I moved to New York to study acting.
A: Where did you study acting?
B: At the Acting Studio. I was there for two years.
A: And then what did you do?
B: Well, then I got my first acting job on TV.

B *Pair work.* Practice the conversation again. Give true information about yourself.

Student A looks at this page. Student B looks at page 76.

A Look at the photos of Laurie and Toshi. Think about the questions you will ask to find the missing information about Toshi. Here are some types of questions you can ask:

When was he...?   *When did he...?*   *How long was he...?*   *How long did he...?*

B *Pair work.* Ask your partner questions about Toshi. Fill in the missing information.

Dawson, L.

Name: Laurie Dawson
Job: Manager
Birthday: March 19, 1977
Birthplace: Los Angeles, USA
Other information:
- graduated from Stanford University in 1998
- worked as a tour guide 1998–2004
- studied Chinese 1999–2004
- lived in Taiwan 2002–2004
- moved to New York in 2004

Yamada, T.

Name: Toshi Yamada
Job: Sports instructor
Birthday: _____
Birthplace: Kobe, Japan
Other information:
- attended language school in the US _____
- worked at a hotel _____
- lived in Sapporo _____
- moved to Tokyo _____
- won a judo tournament _____

C *Pair work.* Look at the information about Laurie. Answer your partner's questions.

Extra

Talk about your past habits and experiences. Use *used to* with the verbs below. Partners ask questions with *how long*. Take turns.

have	go	live	play
read	study	use	

A: *I used to have a cat.*
B: *How long did you have a cat?*
A: *I had a cat for five years.*

Stories

ghost story

fairytale

mystery

science fiction story

fable

western

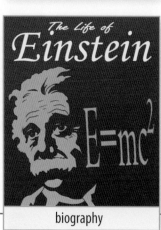
biography

romance

1 Speaking

 Class CD2
Track 34

A Listen and look at the pictures. Then practice with a partner.

A: What kind of story is this?
B: It's a ghost story.

> I like ghost stories.
> I don't like…

B What kinds of stories do you like? What kinds don't you like?
Tell your partner.

2 Listening

 Class CD2
Track 35

People are reading stories. What kind of stories are they? Listen and check (✓) the correct answer.

1. **a.** ❏ fable
   b. ❏ biography

2. **a.** ❏ mystery
   b. ❏ fairytale

3. **a.** ❏ ghost story
   b. ❏ fable

4. **a.** ❏ biography
   b. ❏ science fiction story

5. **a.** ❏ western
   b. ❏ romance

6. **a.** ❏ science fiction story
   b. ❏ fairytale

3 Grammar: *Reported speech* Class CD2 Track 36

Listen. Then listen again and repeat.

Direct statements	Reported statements
"**I'm** tired of ghost stories," he said.	He **said** he **was** tired of ghost stories. He **told** her he **was** tired of ghost stories.
"I **can't** stand mysteries," he said.	He **said** he **couldn't** stand mysteries. He **told** her he **couldn't** stand mysteries.
"Mika **read** Einstein's biography," he	He **said** Mika **had read** Einstein's biography. He **told** her Mika **had read** Einstein's biography.
"**I've seen** that western," he said.	He **said** he **had seen** that western. He **told** her he **had seen** that western.
Direct questions and commands	**Reported questions and commands**
"**Are** you **reading** a fable?" she said.	She **asked** me if I **was reading** a fable.
"**Can** you **read** a fairytale to me?" he said.	He **asked** me **to read** a fairytale to him.
"**Don't read** westerns," she said.	She **told** me **not to read** westerns. She **said not to read** westerns.

> **Memo**
>
> You can use *that* to introduce reported statements: He said **that** *he was tired.* He told her **that** *he couldn't stay.*

4 Conversation Class CD2 Track 37

A   *Pair work.* Listen to the conversation. Then practice with a partner.

A: Hi, Jill. It's Ben.

B: Oh, hi, Ben. Say, have you written your paper for history class yet?

A: Not yet. I'm reading a great biography right now. Look, are you free tomorrow night? I'd like to go over my notes with you.

B: Sorry, but I'm busy. My professor asked me to make a list of mystery novels for my writing class.

A: Oh, that's right! You told me you were doing that. But you said he asked you to research westerns.

B: He did, but last week he said his plans had changed.

A: Well, maybe we can work on the history paper next week.

B   *Pair work.* Practice the conversation again. Use your imagination and change the information.

A Look at the pictures. Who are the people? What happened? What did they do and say? You can put the pictures in any order to tell your story. Number the pictures from 1 to 8. Then think about how you will tell your story. Is the story a romance, a mystery, or a biography?

B *Pair work.* Tell your story to a partner. Take turns.

Extra

Work with your partner. Make up a new story based on the pictures. Tell your story to another pair.

Helpful Language

- First…
- Next…
- Then…
- Finally…

In the news

a flood

a fire

a crime

a demonstration

an election

a sports event

a fashion show

an exhibition

6 Speaking
Class CD2
Track 38

A Listen and look at the pictures. Then practice with a partner.

A: What happened?
B: There was a flood.

B Have you heard or read about a news event recently? Tell your partner.

> I read about a crime. It happened...

7 Listening
Class CD2
Track 39

A Listen to the news reports. What is each report about? Number the events from 1 to 5.

_____ a flood   _____ a fire   _____ an exhibition
_____ a sports event   _____ a fashion show

B Listen again. Are these statements true or false? Check (✓) the correct answer.

	True	False
1. There were a lot of people in the theater.	❑	❑
2. Over 800 people attended the event.	❑	❑
3. The event happened last Friday.	❑	❑
4. The event was held in Boston.	❑	❑
5. The highway was blocked for two hours.	❑	❑

8 Grammar: While *and* then *in clauses*

A Listen. Then listen again and repeat.

> I listen to sports events **while** I'm driving.
>
> We'll go to the fashion show **while** you attend the exhibition.

Memo
Use while to mean during the time that.

> We usually vote in the election, and **then** watch the results on TV.
>
> It rained for three days, and **then** there was a flood.

Memo
Use then before an event that follows a previous event.

B *Pair work.* Tell your partner about things you usually do. Use *while* or *then*. Ask each other follow-up questions.

> I usually sing while I'm taking a shower.

> What songs do you sing?

9 Conversation

A *Pair work.* Listen to the conversation. Then practice with a partner.

A: Where have you been? I've been waiting for almost an hour!

B: I'm sorry I'm late. It started to rain while I was leaving home, so I went back to get an umbrella. Then there was a flood on the highway, and I had to get out of my car. I fell down and hurt my leg while I was running for the bus.

A: Oh, no! How's your leg now?

B: It hurts a little, but I think it's going to be OK. I really am sorry I'm so late.

A: That's OK. But I *was* getting worried. I tried to watch TV while I was waiting for you, but I was too nervous. Anyway, you're here now. That's the important thing.

B *Pair work.* Practice the conversation again. Use different excuses for being late.

A Choose one of the pictures and write a short story about it. Answer the five questions below to get started. Make brief notes about your answers.

What happened?
Who was involved?
When did it happen?
Where did it happen?
Why did it happen?

B *Pair work.* Tell your story to your partner. Your partner asks questions to get more information about the event. Take turns.

Extra

Work with your partner. Write a new story based on another one of the pictures. Read your story to another pair.

Before you travel

buy a plane ticket

PASSPORT PHOTOS

get a passport

TONY MARTIN 10 GREEN ST.

label your luggage

I'd like to reserve a room.

make a hotel reservation

I'm calling to confirm my flight to Bangkok.

BLUE JET AIRLINES

confirm a flight

TRAVELER'S CHECKS

get traveler's checks

1 Speaking
 Class CD2 Track 42

A Listen and look at the pictures. Then practice with a partner.

> A: What's he doing?
> B: He's buying a plane ticket.

B Have you ever done any of these things? Which ones? When? Tell your partner.

> **I bought a plane ticket three weeks ago.**

2 Listening
Class CD2 Track 43

People are talking about things they need to do before they travel. What does each person need to do? Write the letter of the correct answer.

1. Catherine needs to ___
2. Sam needs to ___
3. Jan needs to ___
4. Ron needs to ___
5. Emma needs to ___
6. Lily needs to ___

a. label her luggage
b. confirm a flight
c. pay for a plane ticket
d. make a hotel reservation
e. get a new passport
f. get traveler's checks

Listen. Then listen again and repeat.

Statements in the present	
I **have to** get a passport.	I **don't have to** get a visa.
He **has to** pack.	He **doesn't have to** buy a plane ticket.
I**'ve got to** change money.	She**'s got to** make a hotel reservation.
You **must** bring your passport.	
Statements in the past	
I **had to** get a new passport.	I **didn't have to** get a visa.

Memo

• You can use *have to, have got to* and *must* to say that it is necessary to do something.

• *Have to* is the most common way to express necessity.

• *Have got to* is more informal than *have to.*

• *Must* is used for orders and strong suggestions and advice.

4 **Conversation**   Class CD2
Track 45

A *Pair work.* Listen to the conversation. Then practice with a partner.

A: So when are you leaving for Brazil?

B: Next week. I've finished almost everything I had to do.

A: What did you have to do?

B: A lot of things. I had to buy a plane ticket, of course. And my old passport expired, so I had to get a new one. And this morning I have to go to the Brazilian consulate.

A: Why do you have to go there?

B: I have to get a visa to visit Brazil.

A: When are you going to the consulate?

B: Right now. Look, I'm sorry, but I've got to hang up. It's almost 11:00, and I have to get to the consulate before noon.

A: OK. Bye.

B: Bye. I'll call you when I get back.

B *Pair work.* Practice the conversation again. Use your imagination and change the information.

A *Pair work.* Help your partner make a "to do" list of 7 or 8 important tasks for this week. Ask about *things that have already been done* and *things that haven't been done yet.* Ask for as much information as possible. Check (✓) the things your partner has already done. Take turns.

> A: *Do you have to do anything for school this week?*
> B: *I have to study for an exam.*
> A: *In what subject?*
> B: *Biology.*
> A: *Uh-huh. Who will you study with?*
> B: *I've got to call Brenda and ask her to meet me at the library. I've already reviewed my notes.*

B *Class activity.* Tell the class your partner's tasks for this week. What does he or she have to do? What doesn't he or she have to do? Give as much information as possible about each task.

> *Kenji has to study for a biology exam this week. He is going to study with Brenda. He's got to call and ask her to meet him at the library. He doesn't have to review his notes. He did that yesterday.*

Travel experiences

lose your wallet

travel alone

try local food

lose your passport

visit a local market

take a cruise

miss a flight

run out of money

6 Speaking
Class CD2
Track 46

A Listen and look at the pictures. Then practice with a partner.

> A: Did he lose his wallet?
> B: Yes, he did.

B Which things do you think are a problem? Which things do you think are fun? Tell your partner.

> Losing your wallet is a problem. Traveling alone is…

7 Listening
Class CD2
Track 47

A People are calling home and leaving messages while they are traveling. Which message does each person leave? Listen and circle the correct words.

1. Jim <u>missed a flight / lost his passport</u>.
2. Cara <u>ran out of money / lost her wallet</u>.
3. Ken <u>is traveling alone / is taking a cruise</u>.
4. Tracey <u>tried local food / visited a local market</u>.
5. Alex lost his <u>passport / plane ticket</u>.
6. Katie <u>ran out of money / missed a flight</u>.

B Listen again. Circle T for true or F for false.

1. Jim will call again tonight.   T   F
2. Cara has her credit cards   T   F
3. Ken will send a postcard.   T   F
4. Tracey was tired of fast food.   T   F
5. Alex got a boarding pass.   T   F
6. Katie is having a good time.   T   F

A Listen. Then listen again and repeat.

Have you **tried** the local food?	Yes, **I have**. **I've tried** the local food.
How many times **have** you **missed** a flight?	**I've missed** one flight.
Have you ever **traveled** alone?	**I've traveled** alone three times.
Have you ever **been** to a local market?	No, **I haven't**. **I've never been** to a local market.
What's the biggest country you**'ve visited**?	The biggest country **I've visited** is China.

Memo
- Use the present perfect to talk about a period of time that continues up to the present.
- We often use the present perfect with *ever* after a superlative: *It was the best trip I've ever taken.*

B *Pair work.* Ask your partner questions about things he or she has done. Use the ideas below or your own idea.

ever / see / animated movie   ever / met / famous person
how many times / be / in love   what / most beautiful city / ever / visit

Have you ever been to Singapore?   **No, I haven't.**

A *Pair work.* Listen to the conversation. Then practice with a partner.

A: Have you traveled a lot, Julia?
B: Yes, I have. I've been to 30 different countries.
A: Thirty different countries! That really is a lot. Have you ever gotten sick on a trip?
B: Oh, yes. I've had accidents, too, but I'd never stop traveling. In fact, I've traveled alone a lot. People are friendly to travelers. They always help you.
A: What's the worst thing that's ever happened to you?
B: I lost my passport, and I ran out of money one time. That's the worst so far. But I've never missed a flight. What about you? Have you had good luck traveling?
A: Yes, I have, but I haven't traveled as much as you have.

B *Pair work.* Practice the conversation again. Use your imagination and talk about different experiences.

A   *Class activity*. Ask questions with *Have you ever…?* Find a classmate for each activity.
Write your classmates' names and any extra information.

A: *Have you ever visited an island?*
B: *Yes, I have.*
A: *What island did you visit?*
B: *I visited Guam.*
A: *When did you go there?*
B: *I went there two years ago.*

has visited an island.
(Find out what island
and when.)

has gone on a cruise.
(Find out how many times
and where.)

has traveled alone.
(Find out where and when.)

has missed a flight.
(Find out where and when.)

has lost a plane ticket.
(Find out where and when.)

has taken a cruise.
(Find out where and when.)

has run out of money
on a trip.
(Find out where and when.)

has gotten sick on a trip.
(Find out where and when.)

has eaten something
unusual on a trip.
(Find out what and where.)

has taken a lot of photos
on a trip.
(Find out where and when.)

has had an accident on a trip.
(Find out what kind
and where.)

has traveled with a group.
(Find out where and when.)

B   *Group work*. Work in a group of three or four students. Take turns. Talk about
different classmates and the things they have done. Tell as many details as you can.

Akemi has visited an island. She went to Guam two years ago. She…

Student B looks at this page. Student A looks at page 9.

A *Pair work.* Ask your partner the questions in the list below. Use the comparative form of the adjectives in parentheses.

B: *Which continent is ___bigger___, Africa or Asia? (big)*
A: *Asia is bigger than Africa.*

1. Which continent is _____, North America or South America? (large)

2. Which country's population is _____, Indonesia's or Brazil's? (small)

3. Which river is _____, the Nile or the Yangtze? (long)

4. Which river is _____, the Yangtze or Congo? (short)

5. Which ocean is _____, the Indian or the Arctic? (deep)

6. Which republic is _____, Portugal or France? (old)

B *Pair work.* Look at the web page below. Your partner will ask you questions about the items on the web page. Use the information to answer your partner's questions.

A: *Which ocean is bigger, the Pacific or the Atlantic?*
B: *The Pacific is bigger than the Atlantic.*

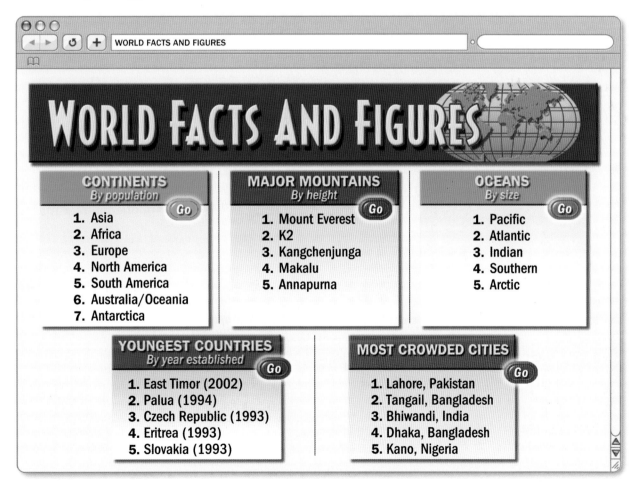

WORLD FACTS AND FIGURES

CONTINENTS
By population
1. Asia
2. Africa
3. Europe
4. North America
5. South America
6. Australia/Oceania
7. Antarctica

MAJOR MOUNTAINS
By height
1. Mount Everest
2. K2
3. Kangchenjunga
4. Makalu
5. Annapurna

OCEANS
By size
1. Pacific
2. Atlantic
3. Indian
4. Southern
5. Arctic

YOUNGEST COUNTRIES
By year established
1. East Timor (2002)
2. Palua (1994)
3. Czech Republic (1993)
4. Eritrea (1993)
5. Slovakia (1993)

MOST CROWDED CITIES
1. Lahore, Pakistan
2. Tangail, Bangladesh
3. Bhiwandi, India
4. Dhaka, Bangladesh
5. Kano, Nigeria

Student B looks at this page. Student A looks at page 27.

Pair work. Look at the conversations below. You have directions for part B of the conversations, and your partner has directions for part A. Role-play the conversations. Use *can, will, could,* and *would* in requests.

Conversation 1

A: ....
B: Ask to speak to Erin.
A: ....
B: Say yes. Tell A your name, and ask A to tell Erin you called to invite her to a party.
A: ....
B: Say thank you and end the call.

Conversation 2

B: Answer the phone.
A: ....
B: Say Yoji is out right now. Ask A if you can give Yoji a message.
A: ....
B: Agree and ask who is calling.
A: ....
B: Say you'll give the message to Yoji.
A: ....

Conversation 3

A: ....
B: Ask to speak to Tasha.
A: ....
B: Say who you are. Ask A to please tell Tasha you're sorry you missed your appointment with her.
A: ....
B: Say thank you. Ask if you can leave your phone number for Tasha.
A: ....
B: Give your phone number.
A: ....

Extra

Think of an unusual request. Call your partner and make your request. Role-play the conversation. Take turns calling and making your requests.

A: *Hi, Miko. This is Frank.*
B: *Oh, hi, Frank. How are you?*
A: *I'm fine, thanks. I'm calling to ask something.*
B: *Sure, what is it?*
A: *Well, could you please...?*

Student B looks at this page. Student A looks at page 39.

A *Pair work.* You and your partner each have a different version of the quiz below. Your partner will read six statements. Listen and say whether you think each statement is true or false.

B *Pair work.* Look at the quiz below. Read each statement to your partner. Your partner says whether the statement is true or false. Check (✓) the answer your partner thinks is correct for each statement.

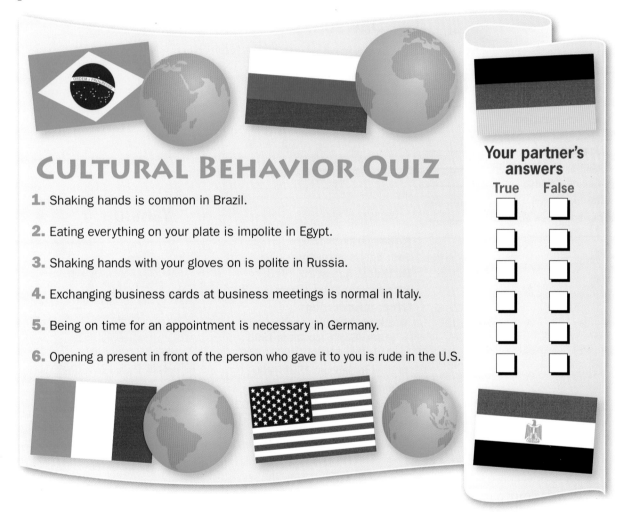

CULTURAL BEHAVIOR QUIZ

Your partner's answers
True　False

1. Shaking hands is common in Brazil.
2. Eating everything on your plate is impolite in Egypt.
3. Shaking hands with your gloves on is polite in Russia.
4. Exchanging business cards at business meetings is normal in Italy.
5. Being on time for an appointment is necessary in Germany.
6. Opening a present in front of the person who gave it to you is rude in the U.S.

C *Pair work.* Here are the correct answers to the statements above: 1T, 2T, 3F, 4T, 5T, 6F. Tell your partner the correct answer for each statement. Take turns.

D *Group work.* Get together with another pair. Ask and answer these questions:

Which of these behaviors are OK to do in your country?
Which behaviors are rude?
Which ones have you done?
Which ones have you seen or heard other people do?

Student B looks at this page. Student A looks at page 60.

A Look at the photos of Laurie and Toshi. Think about the questions you will ask to find the missing information about Laurie. Here are some types of questions you can ask:

Where was she...?   *When did she ...?*   *How long was she ...?*   *How long did she...?*

B *Pair work.* Look at the information about Toshi. Answer your partner's questions.

Dawson, L.

Name: Laurie Dawson
Job: Manager
Birthday: March 19, 1977
Birthplace: _____
Other information:
● graduated from Stanford University _____
● worked as a tour guide _____
● studied Chinese _____
● lived in Taiwan _____
● moved to New York _____

Yamada, T.

Name: Toshi Yamada
Job: Sports instructor
Birthday: August 20, 1973
Birthplace: Kobe, Japan
Other information:
● attended language school in the US for 6 months in 1995
● worked at a hotel 1997–1999
● lived in Sapporo 1999–2001
● moved to Tokyo in 2001
● won a judo tournament in 2003

C *Pair work.* Ask your partner questions about Laurie. Fill in the missing information.

> **Extra**
>
> Talk about your past habits and experiences. Use *used to* with the verbs below. Partners ask questions with *how long*. Take turns.
>
> | | | | |
> |---|---|---|---|
> | *have* | *go* | *live* | *play* |
> | *read* | *study* | *use* | |
>
> **A:** *I used to have a cat.*
> **B:** *How long did you have a cat?*
> **A:** *I had a cat for five years.*

Check your English _____

Unit 1

A Vocabulary

Complete the sentences. Use the words below.

band	camping	generous	serious
shy	talented	talkative	team

1. We went _____camping_____ in the mountains on our last vacation.

2. He never smiles or tells a joke. He's a very _____ person.

3. She's a very _____ musician. She plays the violin and the piano.

4. My father played on a baseball _____ when he was in school.

5. Bob is very _____. He's always giving gifts to people.

6. I'd like to meet her, but I'm too _____ to introduce myself.

7. She plays the drums in a girls' rock _____.

8. He's the most _____ person I know. He always has something to say.

B Grammar

Complete the conversations. Use the correct form of the verbs in parentheses.

1. **A:** Where _____did_____ you _____go_____ last night? (go)

   B: I _____ to the movies with Jung. (go)

2. **A:** What _____ she _____ right now? (do)

   B: She _____ on the phone. (talk)

3. **A:** _____ he smart? (be)

   B: Oh, yes. He _____ five languages! (speak)

4. **A:** _____ you ever _____ to Guam? (be)

   B: No, I _____ . But I'd like to go there. (have)

5. **A:** When _____ you last _____ Chinese food? (eat)

   B: Yesterday. I _____ lunch in a Chinese restaurant. (have)

Check your English _____

Unit 2

A   Vocabulary

Read the definitions. Write the correct words.

forest   desert   island   lake
ocean   valley   volcano   waterfall

1. a mountain that forces hot gas and rocks through a hole at the top: _____

2. water that falls straight down over a rock or from the top of a mountain: _____

3. a large area of land where it is always hot and dry and there is a lot of sand: _____

4. a large area of land that is covered by trees: _____

5. an area of low land between hills or mountains: _____

6. a piece of land completely surrounded by water: _____

7. a large area of water surrounded by land: _____

8. one of the extremely large areas of salt water that cover most of the earth: _____

B   Grammar

Write the comparative or superlative form of the adjective in parentheses, whichever is more appropriate.

1. A stream is _____ than a river. (narrow)

2. The Pacific is _____ ocean on Earth. (deep)

3. A mountain is _____ than a hill. (big)

4. Mount Everest is _____ mountain on Earth. (high)

5. Mount Fuji is _____ than Mount Yahiko. (famous)

6. The weather today is _____ than it was yesterday. (good)

7. The Atacama Desert is _____ place in Chile. (dry)

8. What do you think is _____ city in the world? (interesting)

Check your English

Unit 3

A   Vocabulary

Complete the sentences. Use the words below. Use each word only once.

do   clean   get   have
feed   visit   practice   win

1. She and Charlie are going to _____ married in April.

2. The dog is really hungry. Would you please _____ him?

3. She hoped to _____ a prize in the flower show.

4. Ron can't go out tonight. He has to _____ his homework.

5. Be careful on that bike! You don't want to _____ an accident.

6. My room is a mess. Will you help me _____ it?

7. Do you _____ the piano every day?

8. I went to Seattle to _____ my cousins.

B   Grammar

Complete these sentences with the verbs in parentheses. Use the correct tense: simple past or past continuous.

1. I _____ (walk) home when, suddenly, it _____ (start) to rain.

2. We _____ (see) an accident while we _____ (stand) at the bus stop.

3. My cell phone _____ (fall) on the floor while I _____ (get) dressed.

4. He _____ (watch) TV when his mother _____ (call).

5. He _____ (stay) in a hotel when the tsunami _____ (hit) the beach.

6. When my friend _____ (arrive), I _____ to music (listen).

7. They _____ (meet) the president while they were on vacation.

8. While we _____ (walk) on the beach, we _____ (find) something valuable.

Check your English _____

Unit 4

A   Vocabulary

1   Complete the sentences. Use the words below. Use each word only once.

ask   missed   fail   study

1. Do you _____ the teacher questions in class?

2. I _____ class yesterday because I was sick.

3. You need to _____ these pages for the test.

4. I feel bad when I _____ a test.

2   Match the subjects with the topics.

1. biology ___   **a.** grammar

2. history ___   **b.** $5x + 7y = 12z$

3. languages ___   **c.** plants and animals

4. math ___   **d.** the 18th century

B   Grammar

1   Circle the correct word to complete each sentence.

1. My biology class is always very <u>interesting / interested</u>.

2. She was very <u>exciting / excited</u> about her new job.

3. I was <u>shocking / shocked</u> to hear about the accident.

4. I thought the movie was very <u>boring / bored</u>.

2   Put the words in order to make sentences.

1. called   yet   father   me   hasn't   my

   _____

2. already   eaten   in   have   that   they   restaurant

   _____

Check your English

Unit 5

A Vocabulary

Fill in the blanks with the correct words.

apology   invitation   offer   save a seat
request   suggestion   lend   pick up

1. Eva didn't get a(n) _____ to David's party.

2. He made a(n) _____ for missing the meeting.

3. Akiko's idea to leave early was a good _____.

4. The bank refused my _____ for a loan.

5. Will you _____ something for dinner on your way home?

6. I was very pleased by her _____ to help with the work.

7. He asked me if I would _____ him my bike.

8. Would you please _____ for me at the movie theater?

B Grammar

Circle the correct word to complete each sentence.

1. Would you mind if I <u>wait / waiting / waited</u> for you outside?

2. Can you please <u>answer / answering / answered</u> the phone?

3. Would you mind not <u>drive / driving / drove</u> so fast?

4. Would you mind <u>spell / spelling / spelled</u> your name for me?

5. Would you mind if I <u>call / calling / called</u> you next week?

6. Would you <u>say / saying / said</u> that again, please?

7. Would you mind <u>help / helped / helping</u> me wash the dishes, please?

8. Would you please <u>show / showing / showed</u> me how to use this coffee machine?

Check your English

Unit 6

A Vocabulary

Use the clues to complete the crossword puzzle.

Across

1. He'd really like to _____ more people.

4. There are a lot of _____ on TV and radio.

7. Ken is _____ than his brother.

9. I'd like to _____ to another city.

10. I'm against _____ uniforms.

Down

2. You should get out and _____ life more.

3. He has a _____ of a fish on his leg.

5. He wishes he had more _____ to buy things.

6. Cats and dogs are popular _____ in the United States.

8. Do you know _____ to speak Spanish?

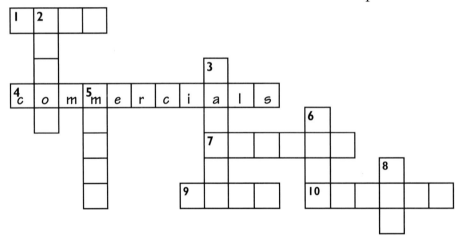

B Grammar

Complete the sentences. Use the words and phrases below.

could stop   enough   many   much   too   would come

1. I smoke too _____ cigarettes. I wish I _____ smoking.

2. I wish Tina _____ to the party.

3. This backpack isn't big _____ to hold all my books.

4. I can't drink this coffee. There's too _____ sugar in it.

5. This food is _____ hot to eat.

Check your English

Unit 7

A Vocabulary

Complete the sentences. Use the words below. Use each word only once.

anniversary	graduation	remove
shake	tip	wedding

1. We had a big party to celebrate my brother's _____ from college.

2. How much did you _____ the taxi driver?

3. The bride and groom are the most important people at a _____.

4. He said, "Nice to meet you" and started to _____ my hand.

5. Next Friday is my parents' wedding _____.

6. You can keep your shoes on. You don't need to _____ them.

B Grammar

1. Make one sentence from two sentences.
   a. People eat dinner in a restaurant. Then they tip the waiter.

      People _tip the waiter_ after _they eat dinner in a restaurant_ .

   b. She graduated. Then she got a good job.
      After _____, _____.

   c. I finished reading the book. Then I had dinner.
      I _____ before _____.

2. Make a sentence with the same meaning. Use a gerund as the subject or *it* + infinitive.
   a. Visiting foreign countries is interesting.

      It's interesting to visit foreign countries. _____

   b. It takes a long time to learn a foreign language.

      _____

   c. Taking a hot bath is relaxing.

      _____

Check your English

Unit 8

A Vocabulary

Match the jobs with the descriptions.

surgeon   hairdresser   firefighter   manager   graphic artist
cashier   photographer   police officer   reporter   mechanic

1. A _____ washes, cuts, and styles people's hair.

2. A _____ takes photos.

3. A _____ repairs and works with machines.

4. A _____ produces art on a computer.

5. A _____ operates on people in a hospital.

6. A _____ tries to catch criminals and checks that people obey the law.

7. A _____ directs the work of a business, department, etc.

8. A _____ puts out fires and helps people in dangerous situations.

9. A _____ receives or gives money in a store, bank, etc.

10. A _____ writes or tells about events in a newspaper or on radio or TV.

B Grammar

Complete each sentence with the infinitive or gerund of the verb in parentheses.

1. She wants _____ the sales meeting. (attend)

2. Do you enjoy _____ new people? (meet)

3. He's really good at _____ reports. (write)

4. I'm planning _____ a job as a manager. (get)

5. Are you interested in _____ part-time? (work)

6. She's really nervous about _____ her new job. (start)

7. I dislike _____ to work. (drive)

8. I'm tired of _____ the same thing every day. (do)

Check your English

Unit 9

A Vocabulary

Complete the sentences. Use the words and phrases below. Use each word or phrase only once.

practice   get   look for   take   train
learn   spend   hang out   build   go

1. How long did you _____ for the race?

2. I want to _____ ice-skating lessons.

3. Who did you _____ to the concert with?

4. He's been trying to _____ how to cook Chinese food.

5. She doesn't have time to _____ another job.

6. They usually _____ at the mall with their friends.

7. Will you help me _____ my website?

8. In the summer she likes to _____ a lot of time at the beach.

9. You look tired. You need to _____ more sleep.

10. I _____ martial arts two days a week.

B Grammar

Complete the conversation using the words in parentheses. Use the present perfect or the present perfect continuous.

A: (1) _____ you in a long time. (I/not/see)

What (2) _____ lately? (you/do)

B: Oh, not much really. (3) _____ a lot. (I/study)

A: Really? Me, too. I have a paper due next week.

(4) _____ all my time at the library. (I/spend)

B: Me, too. (5) _____ to the library three times this week. (I/be)

Check your English

Unit 10

A Vocabulary

Read the sentences. Complete the words.

1. I try to keep my room ___ ___ ___ ___ and clean at all times.

2. The actor wore a thick, black ___ ___ ___ ___ ___ ___ ___ ___ on his face.

3. She just sits in front of the TV all day. She's very ___ ___ ___ ___.

4. The old man had a long, gray ___ ___ ___ ___ ___.

5. You need some new clothes. You look ___ ___ ___ ___ ___ ___ ___ in those.

6. She's a strong athlete. Her body is very ___ ___ ___ ___ ___ ___ ___ ___.

7. My father has no hair on his head. He's completely ___ ___ ___ ___.

8. Her hair isn't straight. It's very long and ___ ___ ___ ___.

9. He's a good worker. I'm ___ ___ ___ ___ ___ ___ ___ ___ ___ that he can do the job.

10. She's always in the library. She's very ___ ___ ___ ___ ___ ___ ___ ___.

B Grammar

Complete the conversation. Use each word or phrase below only once.

did	didn't	for	from	how long
to	until	use	use to	used to

A: Did you **(1)** _____ ride your bike to school?

B: No, I **(2)** _____. I **(3)** _____ ride my skateboard. How did you go to school? Did you **(4)** _____ the subway?

A: Yes, I **(5)** _____. I went to school by subway when I lived in New York.

B: **(6)** _____ did you live in New York?

A: I lived there **(7)** _____ four years. I lived there **(8)** _____ I graduated from high school.

B: What years were you there?

A: I was there **(9)** _____ 2001 **(10)** _____ 2005.

Check your English

Unit 11

A Vocabulary

Match the words with the definitions.

1. biography ___   **a.** a children's story in which magical things happen

2. crime ___   **b.** when people vote for or against someone

3. demonstration ___   **c.** a book that tells the story of a person's life

4. election ___   **d.** a public show of opinion, especially against something

5. exhibition ___   **e.** a story about love between two people

6. fable ___   **f.** a story about a question that is difficult to solve

7. fairytale ___   **g.** an action that is against the law, such as stealing

8. flood ___   **h.** a story about animals that teaches an important lesson

9. mystery ___   **i.** a lot of water that covers land that is usually dry

10. romance ___   **j.** a showing of paintings, products, etc.

B Grammar

Complete the reported sentences with the correct form of the verb.

1. "I'm late," she said. → She said she _____ late.

2. "You play very well," he said. → He told me I _____ very well.

3. "We're leaving," they told us. → They told us they _____.

4. "He can help," she said. → She said he _____ help.

5. "You don't have enough time," he said. → He told me I _____ enough time.

6. "They've left," she said. → She said they _____.

Check your English

Unit 12

A Vocabulary

Complete the sentences. Use the words and phrases below. Use each word or phrase only once.

label	travel alone	cruise	flight
passport	reservation	confirm	run out of

1. I had to sit in the airport for five hours because I missed my _____.

2. _____ your luggage both inside and outside.

3. The immigration officer asked me where I lost my _____.

4. We got on a big ship and took a ten-day _____ in the Mediterranean.

5. Have you made your hotel _____ yet?

6. I'm going to _____ my flight tomorrow.

7. I asked my sister to go with me because I don't want to _____.

8. Don't worry. If you _____ money, you can use a credit card.

B Grammar

Circle the correct words to complete the sentences.

1. Have you ever <u>visit / visited</u> Europe?

2. She doesn't <u>has / have</u> to pack her backpack.

3. **A:** Have you ever been on a cruise?

   B: No, I have never <u>taken / took</u> a cruise.

4. I <u>haven't / don't have</u> to make a hotel reservation.

5. He didn't <u>have / got</u> to get a new passport.

6. He <u>had to / must</u> take a flight from London yesterday.

7. We didn't <u>have / had</u> to pay for a new ticket.

8. You must <u>show / to show</u> your passport when you enter the country.

Key vocabulary

Here is a list of most of the new words in *Talk Time 3*.

adj = adjective
adv = adverb
n = noun
prep = preposition
pron = pronoun
v = verb

Unit 1

brave *adj*

character *n*
cheerful *adj*
collect things *v*
complaining *n*

date *n*
describe *v*
do arts and crafts *v*

engineering *n*
ever *adv*

foreign *adj*
funny *adj*

generous *adj*
go camping *v*
go rock climbing *v*

hardworking *adj*

joke *n*

kind *adj*
kind of (*informal*)

lazy *adj*

never *adv*

pet *n*
play in a band *v*
play on a team *v*
polite *adj*

serious *adj*
shy *adj*
silly *adj*
smart *adj*
spicy *adj*

talented *adj*
talkative *adj*
Thai *adj*
Thailand *n*

What kind…?

Unit 2

Africa *n*
Amazon *n*
Antarctica *n*
Arctic Ocean *n*
Asia *n*
Atlantic Ocean *n*

better *adj*

climate *n*
cloudy *adj*
cold *adj*
continent *n*
crowded *adj*

desert *n*

Europe *n*
(Mount) Everest *n*

foggy *adj*
forest *n*

geography *n*
Gobi Desert *n*

hill *n*
hot *adj*

Indian Ocean *n*
Indonesia *n*
island *n*

K2 *n*

lake *n*

mountain *n*

Nile River *n*
North America *n*

ocean *n*

Pacific Ocean *n*

quiz *n*

rainy *adj*
river *n*

Sahara Desert *n*
season *n*
snowy *adj*
South America *n*
Spain *n*
stream *n*
sunny *adj*

valley *n*
volcano *n*

waterfall *n*
weather *n*
windy *adj*
winter *n*
worse *adj*

Unit 3

believe *v*

clean one's room *v*
contest *n*

dangerous *adj*
do homework *v*

experience *n*

feed a pet *v*
find something
    valuable *v*

get dressed *v*
get engaged *v*
get married *v*
get off a bus *v*
get on the subway *v*
go on (*idiom*)

have an accident *v*
hope *v*

join *v*

life *n*

meet someone
    famous *v*

midnight   *n*

play basketball   *v*
practice the violin   *v*

right away   (*idiom*)

seem   *v*
semester   *n*
subject   *n*

take a walk   *v*
true   *adj*

visit a friend   *v*
visit a special place   *v*
voice mail   *n*

wait for a bus   *v*
win a prize   *v*
withdraw money   *v*

Unit 4

already   *adv*
amaze   *v*
amuse   *v*
annoy   *v*
art   *n*
art history   *n*
ask questions   *v*

biology   *n*
bored   *adj*
boring   *adj*

chemistry   *n*
computer science   *n*
confused   *adj*
confusing   *adj*

difficult   *adj*
disappoint   *v*

essay   *n*
excite   *v*

fail a test   *v*

history   *n*

interested   *adj*
interesting   *adj*

languages   *n*

math   *n*
miss a class   *v*
music   *n*

shock   *v*
still   *adv*
study for a test   *v*
subject   *n*
surprise   *v*

take a test   *v*
take notes   *v*

vegetarian   *n*

yet   *adv*

Unit 5

anyway   *adv*
apology   *n*

can   *v*
could   *v*

downstairs   *adv*

expect   *v*

favor   *n*

give directions   *v*
give someone a ride   *v*

I'm afraid…   (*idiom*)
invitation   *n*

just in case   (*idiom*)

lend money   *v*

offer   *n*

pick up something (at a store)   *v*

reminder   *n*
request   *n*

save a seat   *v*

suggestion   *n*

wait for someone   *v*
will   *v*
would   *v*
Would you mind…?

Unit 6

against   *adv*
agree   *v*
art gallery   *n*

be taller   *v*

credit card   *n*

depressing   *adj*
disagree   *v*

enjoy life   *v*
enough   *adv*

fast food   *n*
for   *adv*

have money   *v*
household pet   *n*

in my opinion…

know how to dance   *v*

meet people   *v*
move to a new apartment   *v*

opinion   *n*

project   *n*

school uniform   *n*

tattoo   *n*
too   *adv*
TV commercial   *n*

violence   *n*
violent   *adj*

wish   *n*

Unit 7

advice *n*
article *n*

behavior *n*
birthday party *n*
bow *v*
bride *n*

celebration *n*
common *adj*
cultural *adj*
custom *n*
customary *adj*

dinner party *n*
disrespectful *adj*

eat bread *v*
event *n*
exchange *v*

graduation *n*

impolite *adj*

New Year's party *n*

pat *v*

remove shoes *v*
ring *n*

serve *v*
shake hands *v*
smile *v*
snap *v*

tip *v*
touch *v*
typical *adj*

unnecessary *adj*
unusual *adj*
use *v*
use chopsticks *v*

wedding *n*
wedding anniversary *n*
whistle *v*

Unit 8

answer questions *v*
apply *v*
attend meetings *v*

become *v*
business *n*

cashier *n*

dancer *n*

firefighter *n*

graphic artist *n*

hairdresser *n*

interview *n*

job *n*
job opening *n*

manager *n*
mechanic *n*
membership *n*

need to *v*

offer *v*

photographer *n*
plan to *v*
police officer *n*
position *n*

reporter *n*

since *adv*
sports instructor *n*
supervise *v*
surgeon *n*

take business trips *v*
tour guide *n*

use the Internet *v*

work *n*

write reports *v*

Unit 9

build a website *v*

cooking course *n*

daydream *v*
draw *v*
driving lessons *n*

get a lot of sleep *v*
go to concerts *v*
guess *v*

hang out *v*
horseback riding *n*

lately *adv*
learn *v*
leisure *n*
look for a job *v*

martial arts *n*

practice *v*

race *n*
racquetball *n*
recent *adj*
rider *n*

spend time *v*
stable *n*

theme park *n*
train *v*

Unit 10

acting *n*
alarm clock *n*

bald *adj*
beard *n*
by the way… (*idiom*)

change *v*
character *n*
confident *adj*

dream *v*

get up early   *v*
go to bed late   *v*

habit   *n*
hairstyle   *n*
have a big breakfast   *v*

lazy   *adj*
little   *adj*

muscular   *adj*
mustache   *n*

neat   *adj*
newspaper   *n*

personality   *n*

ride a bike   *v*

scruffy   *adj*
shy   *adj*
studious   *adj*

Texas   *n*

used to   *v*

wavy hair   *n*

Unit 11

biography   *n*
busy   *adj*

crime   *n*

demonstration   *n*

election   *n*
exhibition   *n*

fable   *n*
fairytale   *n*
fashion show   *n*
fire   *n*
flood   *n*
free   *adj*

ghost story   *n*

highway   *n*

mystery   *n*

nervous   *adj*
news   *n*

report   *v*
research   *v*
romance   *n*

science fiction story   *n*
sports event   *n*
story   *n*

then   *adv*

western   *n*
What happened?
while   *adv*

Unit 12

buy   *v*

confirm a flight   *v*
consulate   *n*
cruise   *n*

expire   *v*

get sick   *v*

have an accident   *v*

in fact   (*idiom*)

label   *v*
local market   *n*
lose   *v*
luck   *n*
luggage   *n*

make a hotel reservation   *v*
miss a flight   *v*
must   *v*

passport   *n*
plane ticket   *n*

run out of money   *v*

stop   *v*

travel alone   *v*
traveler   *n*
traveler's check   *n*

try local food   *v*

visa   *n*

wallet   *n*